Level 5
Englisch

Übungsheft

INHALT

1 About me

LISTENING

1 Meet Greg and Matilda
1. Greg 2. Greg, Matilda 3. Matilda 4. -

2 Right or wrong?
1. right 2. wrong 3. wrong 4. right 5. right 6. wrong
7. right 8. wrong

3 Sentences
1. D 2. H 3. A 4. G 5. B 6. E 7. C 8. F

READING

1 Facts about Sid
name: Sid
age: four/4
colour: black with white feet
lives: in York/in a white house with a nice garden
family: Mathew and Sarah Jones and their mum and dad
house: white house with nice garden
likes: Mathew's bed, mouse
favourite food: fish

2 Sentences about Sid
1. white feet 2. are twins 3. white house … garden.
4. a cage in his bedroom 5. the mouse. 6. his friends

3 Questions about the text
1. is four years old 2. is cool 3. in Mathew's room
4. a mouse 5. favourite food is fish 6. in the garden

4 My pet (Lösungsvorschlag)
cat, Jones, sleep, fish, garden

WRITING

1 About you
a) + b) eigene Lösungen

2 Daisy (Lösungsvorschlag)
b) My name is Daisy Johnson. I'm twelve years old.
I live in Bristol. I have got a brother and sister and
mum and dad. I have got a dog. His name is Trevor.
My hobbies are reading, skateboarding and football.
My favourite food is pizza. I don't like ice cream.

GRAMMAR

1 Forms of be
a) My name is Tom. My family is from Scotland. We
aren't English, we're Scottish. Billy is our dog. He is
three. How old is your pet? My best friends are Denise
and Tariq. We are twelve years old. Denise's pets are
small. They're birds. Tariq's pet is a cat. It isn't nice.
My sister is Jo. She isn't at my school. She's six. I like
basketball. Are you a basketball fan? I'm not a fan of
football.
b) 1. F 2. D 3. A 4. H 5. B 6. G 7. E 8. C

2 Dennis
I am/'m Dennis. Simon is my friend. We are/'re
football fans. Archie is my dog. He is/'s black and
white. Bill and Ben are my rabbits. They are/'re sweet.
I am/'m twelve. My brother is/'s fourteen. He is/'s not
a football fan.

3 Questions and answers
1. How old are you? – I am/'m eleven years old.
2. Are you from London? – No, I am/'m not.
3. Is your brother eight? – Yes, he is.
4. Is pizza your favourite food? – No, it is not/isn't.
5. Am I your best friend? – Yes, you are.
6. Where is David from? – He is/'s from Scotland.
7. What are your hobbies? – My hobbies are reading
   and swimming.
8. Is your mum a football fan? – Yes, she is.

CHECK

1 Meet Balraj and Fiona
1. Balraj + Fiona 2. Fiona 3. Balraj + Fiona 4. Balraj
5. Fiona 6. Balraj 7. Balraj 8. Balraj + Fiona

2 Bill, Bob and Ben
1. right 2. right 3. wrong 4. right 5. right 6. wrong

3 Harry
My name is Harry Smith. I'm ten years old. I live in
a big house in Manchester. I have got a brother and
a sister. My pets are a dog and two rabbits. My
hobbies are skateboarding and basketball. My
favourite food is bananas.

ISBN 978-3-14-121581-6

ISBN 978-3-14-121581-6

4 Maya

Hi. My name <u>is</u> Maya. I <u>am/'m</u> twelve and I live in Stuttgart. My sisters <u>are</u> twins. They <u>are</u> eight. My favourite hobby <u>is</u> dancing. I <u>am/'m not</u> a football fan, I don't like football. Bananas <u>are not</u> my favourite food, I don't like yellow food. Apples <u>are</u> my favourite food. I love green and red apples.

2 At school

LISTENING

1 Bob and his new friends

1. football (im Hörtext) 2. guitar (nicht im Hörtext)
3. museum (nicht im Hörtext) 4. (gold)fish (im Hörtext)

2 Bob or Samuel?

1. Bob + Samuel 2. Samuel 3. Bob 4. Bob + Samuel
5. Samuel 6. Samuel 7. Bob 8. Bob + Samuel

3 Make sentences.

1. E 2. C 3. F 4. G 5. D 6. A 7. H 8. B

4 Questions

1. They are OK. 2. On Mondays and Fridays.
3. France and Russia. 4. France. 5. Samuel's friend and a good football player. 6. His football shoes.

READING

1 Sarah's timetable

Monday	Tuesday	Wednesday	Thursday	Friday
English	<u>English</u>	history	English	<u>music</u>
history	<u>German</u>	geography	<u>history</u>	maths
B	**R**	**E**	**A**	**K**
<u>maths</u>	maths	drama	<u>maths</u>	geography
<u>maths</u>	science	English	geography	<u>science</u>
L	**U**	**N**	**C**	**H**
music	RE	<u>sport</u>	science	German
<u>art</u>	<u>German</u>	<u>swimming</u>	art	<u>drama</u>

2 Complete the sentences.

1. Sam 2. school 3. timetable 4. football 5. Sam's timetable 6. science homework

3 Questions about Sarah's email

1. Sarah sits next to Anna. 2. Maths is Sarah's favourite subject. 3. Sarah has football training on Wednesday. 4. Friday is the best day. 5. Drama is the last lesson of the week. 6. She does her science homework in the cafeteria.

WRITING

1 Answer Sarah's email (Lösungsvorschlag)

Hi Sarah,
Thanks for your email.
My timetable is good. We have got maths on Monday, Wednesday and Friday. I like Friday best. We have drama, art and music. They are my favourite subjects. I don't like Thursday because we have two German lessons. We have science on Tuesday and Wednesday, that is OK.
What do you do at the weekend? I play football in the park.
Best,
Daniel

2 Paul (Lösungsvorschlag)

Hi Mathew,
How are you? My new school is OK. I have got a friend. His name is Peter. He is a football fan and has a cat. I don't like my timetable. I have English every day. Tuesday is my favourite day because I have sport and drama. I also have football training after school on Tuesday. That is fun. We have Mr Smith for art, he is really cool. He is also my tutor.
Have you got a new football club? Our new trainer is nice.
See you,
Paul

GRAMMAR

1 Forms of have got

a) My name is Tom. We<u>'ve got</u> a dog. He <u>has got</u> three black legs and one white leg. He is three. <u>Have you got</u> pets? We<u>'ve got</u> a big white house. It <u>has got</u> a small garden. My family <u>hasn't got</u> a car. <u>Has your family got</u> a car? We<u>'ve got</u> bikes. I<u>'ve got</u> a blue bike and my brother <u>has got</u> a green bike. My parents <u>haven't got</u> new bikes because they like their old bikes.
b) 1. C 2. H 3. A 4. E 5. B 6. G 7. D 8. F

2 Sentences

1. have got 2. has got 3. hasn't got 4. has ... got; hasn't got 5. have got 6. haven't got 7. has got

8. haven't got

3 What have they got?

1. I have got a dog. 2. She has got a cat. 3. He has got a bike. 4. It has got a fish. 5. They have got a house.

CHECK

1 Brendon's timetable

1. right 2. wrong 3. wrong 4. right 5. wrong 6. right 7. right 8. wrong

2 Sam's email

1. C 2. F 3. A 4. E 5. B 6. D

3 Harry (Lösungsvorschlag)

Hi Dennis,

On Monday and Wednesday I have got football after school. On Tuesday I go skateboarding in the skate park. On Thursday there is a new club. It's cooking. On Friday I have my guitar lesson. That is great. What after school activities have you got?

Best,

Harry

4 Have they got …?

Bob: Have you got a dog, Flora?
Flora: No, I haven't. I have/'ve got a rabbit.
Bob: Has Harry got a dog?
Flora: Yes, he has. Have you got a dog Bob?
Bob: No, I haven't got a dog. I have/'ve got a cat.
Harry: Have you got a skateboard, Bob?
Bob: Yes, I have/'ve got a skateboard.
Harry: Flora has got a skateboard too. Do you want to come to the skate park?
Bob: Yes, please. Thanks.

3 At home

LISTENING

1 It's not fair – Brendon and his jobs at home

1. Brendon 2. Brendon's dad 3. Brendon 4. Brendon's sister 5. Brendon 6. Brendon's sister

2 Right or wrong?

1. wrong 2. wrong 3. wrong 4. right 5. right 6. wrong 7. right 8. right

3 Questions

1. Everything is cool. 2. His brother is too small. 3. Brendon's parents fill the dishwasher. 4. She doesn't want to touch the dirty things. 5. He has got a dog. 6. There are too many things on the floor.

4 Mistakes

1. Brendon has a small brother. 2. Brendon's sister empties the dishwasher. 3. Brendon feeds the dog. 4. Brendon will call James later.

READING

1 Paula's flat

garden
kitchen   living room / dining room
sister's bedroom   bathroom
toilet
Paula's bedroom   parents' bedroom

2 Rooms and furniture (Lösungsvorschlag)

1. shelves, chair 2. chairs, cupboard 3. sofa, lamp, TV

3 Sentences

1. Paula and her family have got a new flat. 2. Paula's cat loves the garden. 3. Paula's family has breakfast at the table. 4. Paula's bedroom is next to the front door. 5. Paula has got a wardrobe for her clothes. 6. Paula lives with her sister and her parents.

4 Questions about the text

1. Paula/She thinks it's amazing. 2. Paula/She has got a garden. 3. From the kitchen and the living room/dining room. 4. Paula's parents (have got the biggest bedroom). 5. It is between Paula's bedroom and her sister's bedroom. 6. There are eight rooms in Paula's flat.

WRITING

1 What is in Max's bedroom?

a) 1. bed 2. shelf 3. desk 4. chair 5. lamp 6. window 7. wardrobe 8. pencil case 9. book 10. apple 11. CD 12. basketball

b) eigene Lösung: Gegenstände sind Maxs Schultasche, ein Sofa, ein Fernsehen und ein Bücherregal

ISBN 978-3-14-121581-6

2 **Where are the things in Max's bedroom?**

1. under 2. on 3. between 4. above 5. behind 6. in
7. on 8. under

3 **Your room**

eigene Lösung

GRAMMAR

1 **The simple present**

a) I always <u>get up</u> 7 o'clock. On school days I <u>have</u>
a shower and <u>go</u> downstairs. First, I <u>feed</u> my pets.
They <u>are</u> very hungry. Then I <u>make</u> breakfast for
everyone. My sister <u>takes out</u> the rubbish and my
brother <u>empties</u> the dishwasher. We <u>have</u> breakfast
together and then my parents <u>fill</u> the dishwasher. We
all <u>leave</u> the house at 8 o'clock. After school I <u>go</u> to
the park with my dog, and we <u>play</u> with his ball. He
<u>doesn't</u> always <u>listen</u>, but he <u>loves</u> the park. My dad
<u>cooks</u> dinner, and we all <u>lay</u> the table. We <u>talk</u> about
our day. I <u>don't do</u> my homework until the evening. I
<u>don't go</u> to bed very early. I <u>watch</u> TV or <u>read</u> a book
before I sleep. What <u>do</u> you <u>do</u> every day?
b) 1. They are very hungry. 2. My sister takes out the
rubbish. 3. He doesn't always listen. 4. I don't go to
bed very early. 5. What do you do every day?

2 **Sentences in the simple present**

I <u>make</u> breakfast for my family every day. I <u>don't</u>
<u>feed</u> the cat or <u>take</u> the dog out, but I <u>talk</u> to the fish.
My brother <u>does</u> those jobs. Before I <u>go</u> to school, I
<u>take out</u> the rubbish and <u>empty</u> the dishwasher. My
sister <u>doesn't like</u> it, but she <u>fills</u> the dishwasher after
breakfast. At the weekend I <u>vacuum</u> the living room
and my brother <u>cleans</u> the bathroom. My sister <u>cooks</u>
the dinner. I <u>don't clean</u> the bathroom or <u>cook</u> dinner.

3 **Questions in the simple present**

1. <u>Does</u> Donald <u>make</u> breakfast? – Yes, he <u>does</u>. 2. <u>Do</u>
his brother and sister <u>take out</u> the rubbish? – No, they
<u>don't</u>. 3. Donald, <u>do</u> you <u>empty</u> the dishwasher? – Yes,
I <u>do</u>. 4. What <u>do</u> you <u>do</u> at the weekend? – I <u>vacuum</u>
the living room. 5. <u>Does</u> your brother <u>clean</u> the
bathroom? – Yes, he <u>does</u>.

CHECK

1 **Rebecca's day**

1. does 2. doesn't 3. does 4. does 5. does
6. doesn't 7. does 8. does

2 **Hannah's house**

1. A

3 **Mark's day (Lösungsvorschlag)**

Mark always makes breakfast. He often feeds the cat.
He doesn't take out the rubbish. He sometimes fills
the dishwasher. He doesn't clean the bathroom. He
never cooks dinner.

4 **Me and my family**

We all <u>have</u> jobs to do at home. My parents <u>get</u> up
first and they <u>use</u> the bathroom. My brother <u>gets</u>
up next. He <u>spends</u> so long in the bathroom. I <u>am</u>
in and out in five minutes. My dad <u>makes</u> breakfast
and my brother <u>lays</u> the table. My mum <u>feeds</u> the cat
and I <u>take</u> the dog for a walk. After breakfast I <u>fill</u> the
dishwasher with the dirty cups and plates. We <u>leave</u>
the house together. I <u>ride</u> my bike to school, I <u>don't</u>
<u>walk</u>. After school my brother <u>empties</u> the dishwasher
and <u>puts</u> the clean things in the cupboards. I <u>vacuum</u>
the living room and bedrooms. My mum <u>cooks</u> dinner
when she <u>comes</u> home from work. We <u>eat</u> together
and <u>talk</u> about the day. We <u>don't watch</u> TV together
and my brother <u>doesn't do</u> his homework. What <u>does</u>
your family <u>do</u> every day?

4 In town

LISTENING

1 **What can I do in my free time?**

a) Sports you hear: 1, 2, 3, 6
b) Eleanor chooses 3 hockey

2 **The right ending**

1. a) 2. c) 3. a) 4. b) 5. b) 6. c)

3 **Missing information**

Sport	Place	Day	Time
swimming	swimming pool	Monday	<u>4 o'clock</u>
hockey	playing field	<u>Tuesday</u>	5 o'clock
tennis	<u>tennis club</u>	Wednesday	3 o'clock
inline skating	park	<u>Thursday</u>	afternoon
football (boys)	<u>gym</u>	Friday	6 o'clock
football (girls)	gym	Tuesday	<u>3 o'clock</u>

b) eigene Lösung

ISBN 978-3-14-121581-6

READING

1 What's missing?

Missing in picture: market (next to playground), sports centre and snack bar (next to swimming pool), museum (near supermarket)

2 Mark's town

1. supermarket 2. market 3. park 4. clothes shop
5. zoo 6. snack bar, sports centre/swimming pool

3 Questions about Mark's town

1. near London in England 2. all the food he needs
3. his friends 4. the clothes shop 5. fresh popcorn
6. the museum

4 Your town

eigene Lösung

WRITING

1 In town

a) 1. E 2. H 3. B 4. F 5. C 6. A 7. G 8. D
b) I meet my friends in the park at the weekend. We take our skateboards and go to the skate park. Next to the park is the swimming pool. We go swimming there in the summer. We sometimes go to the zoo and look at the animals. I like the elephants. We meet at the snack bar after school and have a burger and a drink. There is good music there, too. I don't like the museum. There are lots of things to read about old things. The library is boring – too many books to read. The sports centre is great – football, tennis, squash.

2 Funtown (Lösungsvorschlag)

Funtown is a small town. There is a supermarket and a big park. In the park there is a pond. It's great for families. There is a cinema. It shows old films. The museum is interesting, but the library is boring. There is a market on Saturdays. The food in the snack bar is good. You can meet your friends there. You can do lots of sports at the sports centre.

GRAMMAR

1 The imperative

a) The teacher is in the classroom. He talks to the class.
"Sit down, please. Don't talk to your friends now.

Take out your English books."
"What page do we need?" asks Tom.
"Turn to page 32, please." says the teacher. "Don't open the window, Sarah! It's too cold."
"Sorry, Mr Smith."
"Don't use your phones in lessons. Put them in your schoolbags."
"Don't give us homework today, please. It's Friday."
"OK. No homework today!"
b) Was soll die Klasse tun? Sit down. Take out their English books. Turn to page 32. Put their phones in their schoolbags.
Was soll die Klasse nicht tun? Talk to their friends now. Open the window. Use their phones in lessons. Not get homework.

2 What can you do?

1. Close your book. 2. Open the window, please.
3. Stop at the end of the road. 4. Turn to page 1 in your English book. 5. Don't talk in the library. 6. Don't swim in the river. 7. Don't play football in the car park. 8. Don't take your dog in the sports centre.

3 At home

eigene Lösung

CHECK

1 Sophie's area

1. not in area 2. in area 3. not in area 4. not in area
5. in area 6. in area 7. in area 8. in area

2 My town

1. wrong 2. right 3. right 4. wrong 5. wrong 6. right

3 Free time

There is lots to do in town. You can go to the sports centre and meet your friends at the snack bar. You can play football in the gym or go swimming in the swimming pool. I like the shopping centre, too. You can buy so many things there. There are clothes shops and sweet shops. There is a bike shop with old bikes and new bikes. The market is interesting. It also sells old things like books and clothes. You can buy fresh fruit and vegetables there, too. The park is nice in the summer. There is a skate park and a river with boats. Families like the playground.

ISBN 978-3-14-121581-6

4 Bailey

1. Bailey, sit down! 2. Don't eat my homework, please! 3. Bailey, get your ball! 4. It's hot. Drink your water, Bailey! 5. Don't sleep on my bed, Bailey!

5 Let's celebrate

LISTENING

1 At the shops

a) Food the boys need: 1, 2, 3, 5
b) 1. crisps 2. cake 3. cheese 4. drinks 5. pizza 6. chips

2 The right numbers

1. 8 / eight (16 / sixteen) 2. 45 / forty-five 3. 3 / three 4. £1.50 5. 35 / thirty-five 6. 16 / sixteen 7. 24 / twenty-four 8. 11 / eleven

3 Questions

1. Brendon 2. yes, he has lots 3. on the internet 4. has a special price 5. look good, very small 6. Tom and Oliver 7. two 8. extra cheese and vegetables

READING

1 Samira's list

balloons, ham, cheese, ontions, chocolate cake, lemonade, orange juice

2 Where are the things?

1. F 2. A 3. D 4. H 5. B 6. E 7. C 8. G

3 Questions about Samira's party

1. next week 2. flowers and tomatoes 3. pizzas with cheese, tomatoes, ham and onions 4. a chocolate cake 5. cola, milk, tea and coffee 6. their favourite crisps

4 Food and drink

Food words: pizza, cheese, ham, tomatoes, onions, chocolate cake, biscuits, crisps
Drink words: lemonade, orange juice, cola, milk, tea, coffee

WRITING

1 In the supermarket

This is a picture of a supermarket. There are <u>two</u> people in the supermarket. A <u>girl</u> is looking at the pizzas. A man is looking at the <u>drinks</u> and some bananas. There are lots of shelves in the supermarket. <u>At the back</u> there are two fridges with milk, meat and cheese. <u>On the left</u> there are drinks. I can see orange juice, <u>lemonade</u> and cola. <u>On the right</u> there are sweets, crisps, cakes, biscuits and muesli. There is a man <u>at the bottom</u> of the picture. He is wearing a <u>blue</u> sweatshirt. There is a girl <u>at the back</u> of the picture. She has a blue bag and is wearing a <u>pink</u> sweatshirt, a blue skirt and pink trainers.

2 Playing a game (Lösungsvorschlag)

There two people playing a game. There is a man at the back. He is drinking a glass of lemonade. There are two pictures on the wall. They are pictures of pink flowers. The people are sitting at a table. There are four green chairs in the picture.

GRAMMAR

1 The present progressive

a) It's a nice day and there are lots of people in the park. Let me tell you what <u>they are doing</u>.
There <u>is a man selling</u> ice creams. They look yummy. <u>Two girls are riding</u> their bikes. <u>They are wearing</u> blue helmets.
<u>Six boys are playing</u> football. <u>The red team is winning</u>. <u>A man is taking</u> his big dog for a walk. <u>He is talking</u> to a woman with a small dog. <u>They are laughing</u>. <u>The small dog is barking</u> at the big dog.
<u>A family is eating</u> a picnic. <u>They are sitting</u> on the grass next to the lake. <u>They are celebrating</u> a birthday.
b) 1. The man/He is selling ice creams. 2. The girls/They are wearing blue helmets. 3. The boys/They are playing football. 4. The small dog is barking at the bog dog. 5. The family/They are sitting on the grass (next to the lake). 6. The family/They are eating a picnic/celebrating a birthday.

2 What is happening?

1. is talking 2. is doing 3. isn't smiling 4. are laughing 5. is giving 6. aren't watching

3 What are they doing?

1. The girl <u>is looking at jeans</u>. 2. The man <u>is playing a guitar</u>. 3. The children <u>are singing a song</u>. 4. The people <u>aren't eating ice cream</u>. 5. The girl <u>isn't reading a comic</u>.

ISBN 978-3-14-121581-6

CHECK

1 Sarah's dream birthday party
1. right 2. right 3. wrong 4. right 5. wrong 6. wrong
7. right 8. right

2 My party
right invitation: 2

3 Free time
Ben: Hi Peter. We need to go shopping for my party.
Mo: No problem. I can help. What do you need?
Ben: I want to make pizzas.
Mo: Yummy. We need <u>cheese</u>, <u>tomatoes</u>, <u>salami</u>, ham, …
Ben: I have <u>ham</u>. We don't need to buy it. We need something to drink, too.
Mo: What about <u>lemonade</u> and orange juice?
Ben: Lemonade is my favourite drink. We need to buy some. We have lots of orange juice.
Mo: What about a cake? Do you want to make one?
Ben: Yes, a chocolate cake. We need <u>eggs</u>, <u>butter</u>, flour, sugar and <u>chocolate</u> for the cake.
Mo: Do we need to buy everything?
Ben: No. We have <u>flour</u> and <u>sugar</u> in the cupboard.

4 At the party
1. is sleeping 2. is walking 3. are singing 4. isn't dancing 5. is sitting 6. aren't eating

6 On holiday

LISTENING

1 The United Kingdom
Überprüfe deine Antworten mit Hilfe einer Karte

2 The weather today
1. wrong 2. right 3. right 4. wrong 5. right 6. right 7. wrong 8. right

3 Complete the sentences.
1. England and Wales 2. 18 and 22 degrees 3. of the year 4. east coast 5. the afternoon 6. tomorrow
7. go swimming 8. your garden

4 What's the weather?
1. A, B, C, H 2. A, B, H 3. E, F, G, H 4. D, H

READING

1 Anna's postcard
a) 2 ; b) 3

2 About the postcard
a) 1. wrong 2. right 3. right 4. right 5. wrong 6. wrong
7. right 8. right
b) 1. Anna is on holiday in Brighton. 5. They have made three new friends. 6. They meet them on the beach every morning.

3 Questions about the postcard
1. The weather is great. 2. She goes to the beach.
3. She built a sandcastle. 4. Her new friends are Sarah, Paul and Noah. 5. She eats fish and chips every day. 6. She eats on the beach every day.

WRITING

1 A postcard
a) D, H, C, G, E, B, A, F
b) Hi Sue, I'm on holiday with my family in London. Yesterday we went on a boat trip on the Thames. Today we are going to the Science Museum. Tomorrow we are going to the Tower of London. I'm having a great time here, but we have to leave on Friday. See you at the weekend. Rosie

2 Your postcard (Lösungsvorschlag)
Hi Tom,
I'm on holiday with my family. The weather is cloudy and rainy. The food is good. We saw the mountains and a bear yesterday. We went hiking, kayaking and cycling.
See you on Friday.
Ben

GRAMMAR

1 The simple past
a) I <u>had</u> a great weekend. We <u>went</u> to the mountains for the weekend. We <u>arrived</u> on Friday evening and <u>had</u> a great meal. We all <u>slept</u> really well and <u>got up</u> early on Saturday morning. We <u>got</u> dressed and <u>had</u> a big breakfast. Then we <u>took</u> the bus and <u>walked</u> up a mountain. It <u>was</u> a lovely day and there <u>was</u> a lovely view from the top of the mountain. We decided to come down the mountain in the cable car. On Sunday we <u>met</u> my aunt and uncle and cousins, and we <u>went</u>

ISBN 978-3-14-121581-6

ISBN 978-3-14-121581-6

kayaking all day. We all <u>enjoyed</u> the day together. We <u>came</u> home tired but very happy.

b) 1. had 2. went 3. arrived 4. slept 5. got up 6. took
7. walked 8. was 9. decided 10. met 11. enjoyed
12. came

2   What happened?
1. washed 2. left 3. go 4. moved 5. arrives 6. fell
7. play 8. stayed

3   What did Ben do or not do yesterday?
1. got up 2. didn't eat 3. forgot 4. didn't shout
5. were 6. played 7. didn't miss … was 8. went

4   Questions for Emma
1. When did you eat your breakfast? 2. Where did you watch TV? 3. Did you phone your dad? 4. Did you feed the dog? 5. How did you go to school? 6. What did you do after school? 7. What did you do in the evening? 8. Who did you read a story to?

CHECK

1   Sophia's holiday
1. yes 2. no 3. yes 4. no 5. yes 6. yes 7. yes 8. no

2   Paul's holiday
1. Paul is on holiday in Wales. 2. The weather is awful.
3. He writes about hiking and kayaking. 4. He got wet.
5. The food is good. 6. He doesn't need any lunch.

3   A postcard
We had a great holiday in Scotland. The weather was <u>OK</u>. There was <u>sun</u> and <u>wind</u>, but we did lots of things. I <u>didn't like</u> the food in the hotel. It wasn't very good. We saw lots of things in Scotland. We went to three <u>museums</u>: a science museum, a car museum and a clothes museum. We saw the <u>queen</u> when we went to a farm show. We did lots of <u>walking</u> and we went on a great <u>boat trip</u>. We saw lots of things from the river. It was great.

4   Yesterday
1. went 2. didn't rain 3. was 4. met 5. stayed 6. had
7. didn't see 8. did

INHALT

About me

Audio: (▶) WEBCODE WES-121581-001

1 Meet Greg and Matilda

Which pictures go with Greg and which pictures go with Matilda? Tick ✓ .

Welche Bilder passen zu Greg and welche Bilder passen zu Matilda? Setze Häkchen.

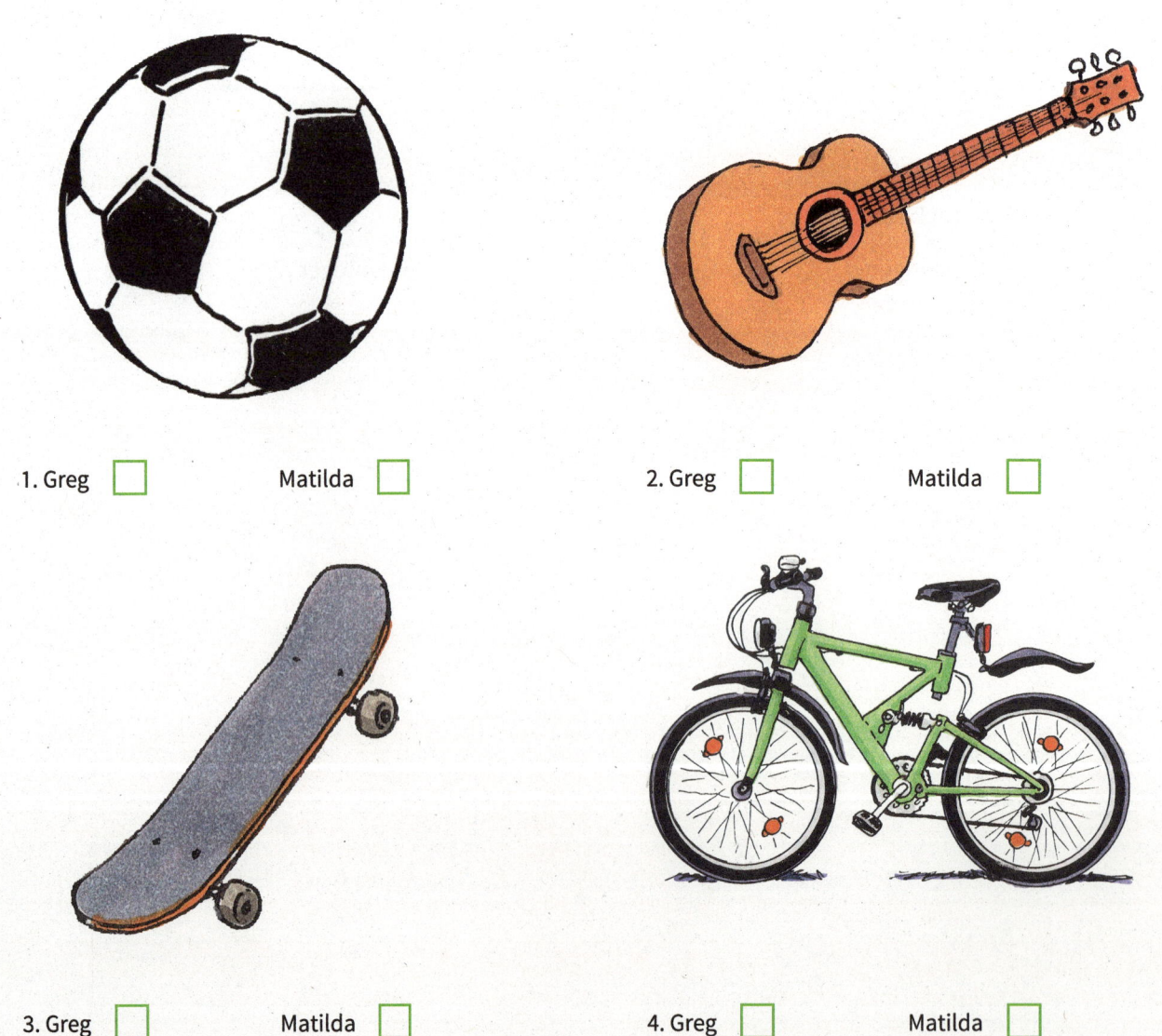

1. Greg ☐   Matilda ☐   2. Greg ☐   Matilda ☐

3. Greg ☐   Matilda ☐   4. Greg ☐   Matilda ☐

Tipp

Jetzt bearbeite diese Aufgaben zum Hörtext über Greg und Matilda. Du darfst den Hörtext vor und nach jeder Aufgabe noch einmal anhören. So kannst du deine Antworten am Ende noch einmal überprüfen.

2 Right or wrong?

Are the sentences right or wrong? Tick ✔ .
Sind die Antworten richtig oder falsch? Setze Häkchen.

	right	wrong
1. Greg lives in Hendon.	☐	☐
2. Greg has got a brother and sister.	☐	☐
3. Greg lives with his father.	☐	☐
4. Greg has got a dog.	☐	☐
5. Matilda lives in Hendon.	☐	☐
6. Matilda's sister is in a wheelchair.	☐	☐
7. Matilda plays the guitar and tennis.	☐	☐
8. Matilda has got a bike and a skateboard.	☐	☐

3 Sentences

Match the sentence parts. Write down the correct letters.
Ordne die Satzteile zu. Schreibe die richtigen Buchstaben auf.

1. Greg's sister	A is Barker.
2. Greg's father lives	B nine years old.
3. Greg's dog	C like dancing.
4. Greg loves	D is Jenna.
5. Matilda is	E a pet.
6. Matilda hasn't got	F food is pizza.
7. Matilda doesn't	G football.
8. Matilda's favourite	H in York.

1	2	3	4	5	6	7	8
D							

Sid the cat

Meow! I'm Sid and I'm four years old. I'm black with white feet.
I live in York. I've got a cool family: Mathew and Sarah Jones and
their mum and dad. Mathew and Sarah are twins.
We live in a white house with a nice garden. I sleep all day in
Mathew's bedroom. He has got a nice bed. He has got a mouse in
a cage in his bedroom. I talk to the mouse. I like the mouse, but
the mouse doesn't like me.
My favourite food is fish. Sarah gives me my food. Then I walk in
the garden and meet my friends. We have fun together.

1 Facts about Sid

Write down the facts about Sid.
Schreibe die Informationen über Sid auf.

name: _Sid_____

age: _____

colour: _____

lives: _____

family: _____

house: _____

likes: _____

favourite food: _____

Tipp

Jetzt bearbeite diese Aufgaben zum Text über Sid. Du darfst den Text vor und nach jeder Aufgabe nochmal lesen. So kannst du deine Antworten am Ende noch einmal überprüfen.

2 Sentences about Sid

Complete the sentences with information from the text.
Vervollständige die Sätze mit den Informationen aus dem Text.

1. Sid is black and has got _____ .

2. Mathew and Sarah _____ .

3. Sid lives in a _____ with a _____ .

4. Mathew has got a mouse in _____ .

5. Sid talks to _____ .

6. Sid has fun with _____ .

3 Questions about the text

Answer the questions.
Beantworte die Fragen.

1. How old is Sid? Sid _____ .

2. What is Sid's family like? Sid's family _____ .

3. Where is Sid's favourite bed? Sid's favourite bed is _____ .

4. What is in the cage in Mathew's bedroom? Mathew has got _____ in the cage.

5. What is Sid's favourite food? Sid's _____ .

6. Where does Sid meet his friends? Sid meets his friends _____ .

4 My pet

Write five words to describe Sid.
Schreibe fünf Wörter auf, die Sid beschreiben.

_____

_____

Tipp

1. In einem Text über eine Person kannst du z.B. über die Familie, Hobbies und Vorlieben schreiben.
2. Sammle Ideen und Wörter zu der Person. Hierzu ist eine Mindmap oder eine Liste hilfreich.
3. Nimm dir einen Mustertext zur Hand. Er hilft dir bei der Formulierung deines Textes.
4. Überlege dir eine Reihenfolge: Was schreibst du zuerst, was folgt darauf und was steht am Ende?
5. Schreibe deinen Text.
6. Lies ihn einmal laut vor und korrigiere deine Fehler.

1 About you

a) Write down some facts about yourself.
Schreibe ein paar Informationen über dich auf.

Facts about me

name: _____   age: _____

live: _____

family: _____

pets: _____

hobbies: _____

favourite food: _____

b) Write a text about yourself. Use the information from a).
Schreibe einen Text über dich. Verwende die Informationen aus a).

My name is _____ . I'm _____ years old.

I live in _____ . I have got _____

_____ and _____ . My hobbies are

_____ .

My favourite food is _____ .

Tipp

Wenn du keine Geschwister oder Haustiere hast, schreib: *no brothers, no sisters* oder *no pets.*

Tipp

Du muss nicht alle Informationen in deinen Text über Daisy schreiben. Wähle das aus, was du wichtig findest.

---

2 Daisy

a) Look at the facts about Daisy.

Schau dir die Fakten über Daisy an.

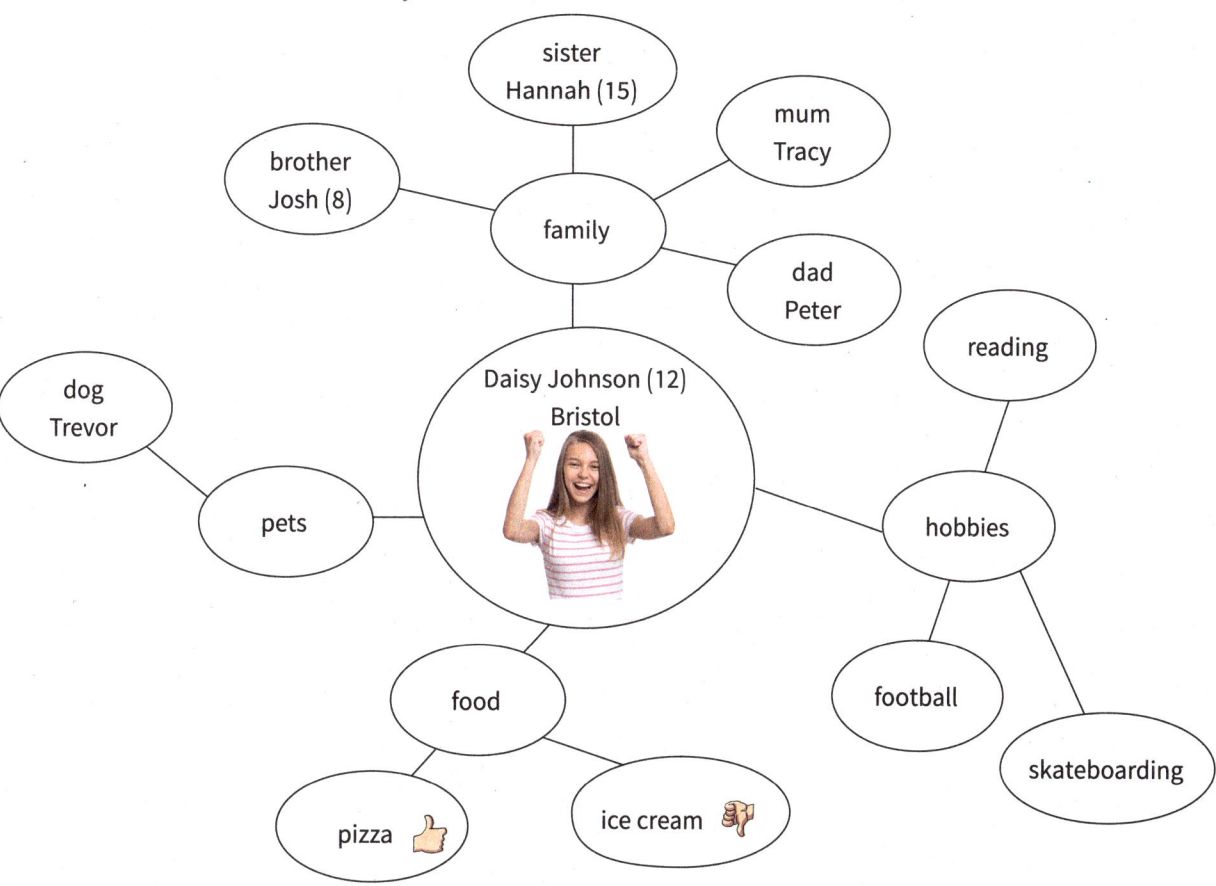

b) Write Daisy's text. Use the information from a).

Schreibe Daisys Text. Verwende die Information aus a).

My name is _____

_____

_____

_____

_____

_____

_____

Language Tip

Das englische Verb für ‚sein' ist **be**.
Es gibt drei Formen: **am**, **is** und **are** sowie Kurzformen. Diese verwendet man beim Sprechen und informellen Schreiben, z. B. bei persönlichen E-Mails und Chats.
Bei der Verneinung verwendet man **not** oder eine Kurzform.

Personalpronomen	Langform	Kurzform	Verneinung	Frage
I	am	I'm	am not/'m not	Where **am** I …?
you, we, they	are	you're/we're/they're	are not/aren't	**Are** you/we/they …?
he, she, it	is	he's/she's/it's	is not/isn't	Who **is** he/she/it …?

Video: ▶ WEBCODE WES-121581-002

1 Forms of *be*

a) Read the text and underline all the forms of *be*. Don't forget the short forms.
   Lies den Text und unterstreiche alle Formen des Verbs be. Vergiss die Kurzformen nicht.

> My name is Tom. My family is from Scotland. We aren't English, we're Scottish. Billy is our dog. He is three. How old is your pet? My best friends are Denise and Tariq. We are twelve years old. Denise's pets are small. They're birds. Tariq's pet is a cat. It isn't nice. My sister is Jo. She isn't at my school. She's six. I like basketball. Are you a basketball fan? I'm not a fan of football.

b) Match the sentences with the German meanings. The underlined parts of the text in a) can help.
   Verbinde die Sätze mit der deutschen Bedeutung. Die unterstrichenen Textteile in a) helfen dir dabei

1. Wir sind nicht Englisch.
2. Er ist drei.
3. Wie alt ist dein Haustier?
4. Wir sind zwölf Jahre alt.
5. Sie sind Vogel.
6. Sie ist nicht an meine Schule.
7. Sie ist sechs.
8. Bist du ein Fußballfan?

A How old is your pet?
B They're birds.
C Are you a football fan?
D He is three.
E She's six.
F We aren't English.
G She isn't at my school.
H We are twelve years old.

1	2	3	4	5	6	7	8
F							

2 Dennis

What does Dennis say? Complete the sentences with *am*, *is* or *are*.
Was sagt Dennis? Setze am, is oder are ein.

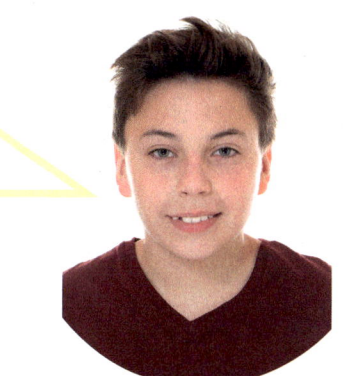

I _____ Dennis. Simon _____ my friend.

We _____ football fans.

Archie _____ my dog. He _____ black

and white.

Bill and Ben _____ my rabbits. They

_____ sweet.

I _____ twelve. My brother _____

fourteen. He _____ not a football fan.

3 Questions and answers

Complete the questions and answers.
Vervollständige die Fragen und Antworten.

1. How old _____ you? – I _____ eleven years old.

2. _____ you from London? – No, _____ .

3. _____ your brother eight? – Yes, _____ .

4. _____ pizza your favourite food? – No, _____ .

5. _____ I your best friend? – Yes, _____ .

6. Where _____ David from? – He _____ from Scotland.

7. What _____ your hobbies? – My hobbies _____ reading and swimming.

8. _____ your mum a football fan? – Yes, _____ .

Audio: ▶ WEBCODE **WES-121581-003**

1 **Meet Balraj and Fiona**

Listen to Balraj and Fiona. Match the things with the right child. Sometimes they match both children.
Höre Balraj und Fiona zu. Ordne die Sachen dem richtigen Kind zu. Manchmal passen sie zu beiden Kindern.

	Balraj	Fiona
1. London		
2. father in Birmingham		
3. twelve		
4. sister		
5. cat		
6. goldfish		
7. basketball		
8. music		

2 **Bill, Bob and Ben**

We're rabbits. Our names are Bill, Bob and Ben. We're two years old. We have got brown ears.
We live in Bristol. Our family is nice.
We live in a cage in Sam's bedroom. We sleep and play all day.
Our favourite food is carrots. Sarah gives us carrots and plays with us. We go in the garden and eat grass. We have fun.

Are the sentences right or wrong? Tick ☑ .
Sind die Antworten richtig oder falsch? Setze Häkchen.

	right	wrong
1. Bill, Bob and Ben have got brown ears.	☐	☐
2. They live in Bristol.	☐	☐
3. They don't like their family.	☐	☐
4. They sleep and play all day.	☐	☐
5. They like carrots.	☐	☐
6. They play with a ball in the garden.	☐	☐

3 Harry

Write Harry's text. Use the information in the box.
Schreibe Harrys Text. Verwende die Informationen aus dem Kasten.

name:	Harry Smith
age:	ten
live:	big house in Manchester
family:	brother, sister
pets:	dog, two rabbits
hobbies:	skateboarding, basketball
favourite food:	bananas

My name is _____ .

I'm _____ years old.

I live in _____ .

I have got _____ and _____ .

My pets are _____ and _____ .

My hobbies are _____ and _____ .

My favourite food is _____ .

3 Maya

Complete the text with the right forms of *be*.
Ergänze den Text mit die richtigen be Formen.

Hi. My name _____ Maya.

I _____ twelve and I live in

Stuttgart. My sisters _____ twins.

They _____ eight.

My favourite hobby _____

dancing. I _____ a football fan, I don't like football. Bananas _____ my

favourite food, I don't like yellow food. Apples _____ my favourite food.

I love green and red apples.

At school

Audio: ▶ WEBCODE WES-121581-004

1 Bob and his new friends

a) Write the words under the pictures.
   Schreibe die Wörter unter die Bilder.

1.   2.   3.   4.

_____   _____   _____   _____

b) Now listen to the text. Which things in a) did you hear in the text? Tick ✓ .
   Höre dir jetzt den Text an. Welche Sachen aus a) hast du in dem Text gehört? Setze Häkchen.

2 Bob or Samuel?

Match the things with Bob or Samuel. Sometimes they match both children.
Ordne die Sachen Bob oder Samuel zu. Manchmal passen sie zu beiden Kindern.

	Bob	Samuel
1. football fan		
2. Arsenal fan		
3. Chelsea fan		
4. goldfish		
5. sister		
6. parents from France		
7. no homework		
8. meet in the park		

Tipp

Du solltest dir einen Text immer mehrmals anhören. Vergiss nicht, deine Antworten am Ende noch einmal zu überprüfen. Höre dir den Text dazu noch einmal an.

3 Make sentences.

Match the sentence parts. Write down the correct letters.
Ordne die Satzteile zu. Schreibe die richtigen Buchstaben auf.

1. The students in Bob's class		A Samuel's sister.
2. There are 12 boys and		B Samuel's friend.
3. Bob sits		C 14 girls in his class.
4. Samuel plays football		D have got goldfish.
5. Samuel and Bob		E are very friendly.
6. Isabella is		F next to Samuel.
7. In the park		G in a football club.
8. Amy is		H they can play football.

1	2	3	4	5	6	7	8
E							

4 Questions

Answer the questions.
Beantworte die Fragen.

1. What are Bob's new teachers like? _____

2. When is football training? _____

3. Where are the two goldfish names from? _____

4. Where are Samuel's parents from? _____

5. What is Amy? _____ and _____

6. What does Bob have to get? _____

Tipp

Um den Text besser zu verstehen, kannst du wichtige Textstellen unterstreichen. In dem Text unten geht es um einen Stundenplan. Wenn du die Schulfächer in rot und die Wochentage in blau unterstreichst, wird dir die Aufgabe im Anschluss leichter fallen.

From:	XXXXXXXXXXXXXXXXXXXXXXXX	✉ @
Reference:	My new school	

Hi Sam,

My new school is great. The students and teachers are really nice. I sit next to Anna. She has got a sister in our class too. How is our old school?

My timetable is OK. On Monday I have my favourite subject maths. Two lessons after break. We also have art in the last lesson. On Tuesday we have English and German before break and German again after lunch before we go home. On Wednesday we have sport after lunch then swimming and I have football training after school. Maths again on Thursday after break and history before break. Friday is the best day: music, drama and science. The last lesson of the week is drama and then it's the weekend. I do my science homework after the lesson at lunch in the cafeteria. Anna helps me. What is your timetable like?

Best,

Sarah

1 ▸ Sarah's timetable

Complete Sarah's timetable with information from her email.
Ergänze Sarahs Stundenplan mithilfe der Informationen aus der E-Mail.

Monday	Tuesday	Wednesday	Thursday	Friday
English		history	English	
history		geography		maths
B	**R**	**E**	**A**	**K**
	maths	drama		geography
	science	English	geography	
L	**U**	**N**	**C**	**H**
music	RE		science	German
			art	

2 Complete the sentences.

Complete the sentences with about 1 to 2 words.
Ergänze die Sätze mit ca. ein bis zwei Wörtern.

1. Sarah's email is to _____ .

2. Sarah goes to a new _____ .

3. Sarah writes about her _____ .

4. After school Sarah plays _____ .

5. Sarah asks about _____ .

6. Anna helps Sarah with her _____ .

3 Questions about Sarah's email

Answer the questions.
Beantworte die Fragen.

1. Who does Sarah sit next to? _____

2. What is Sarah's favourite subject? _____

3. When does Sarah have football training? _____

4. Which day is the best day? _____

5. What is the last lesson of the week? _____

6. Where does Sarah do her science homework? _____

Tipp

Wenn du eine E-Mail beantwortest, unterstreiche am besten die Fragen, auf die du antworten möchtest.

Vergiss nicht, dir deinen Text am Ende noch einmal laut vorzulesen und Fehler zu korrigieren.

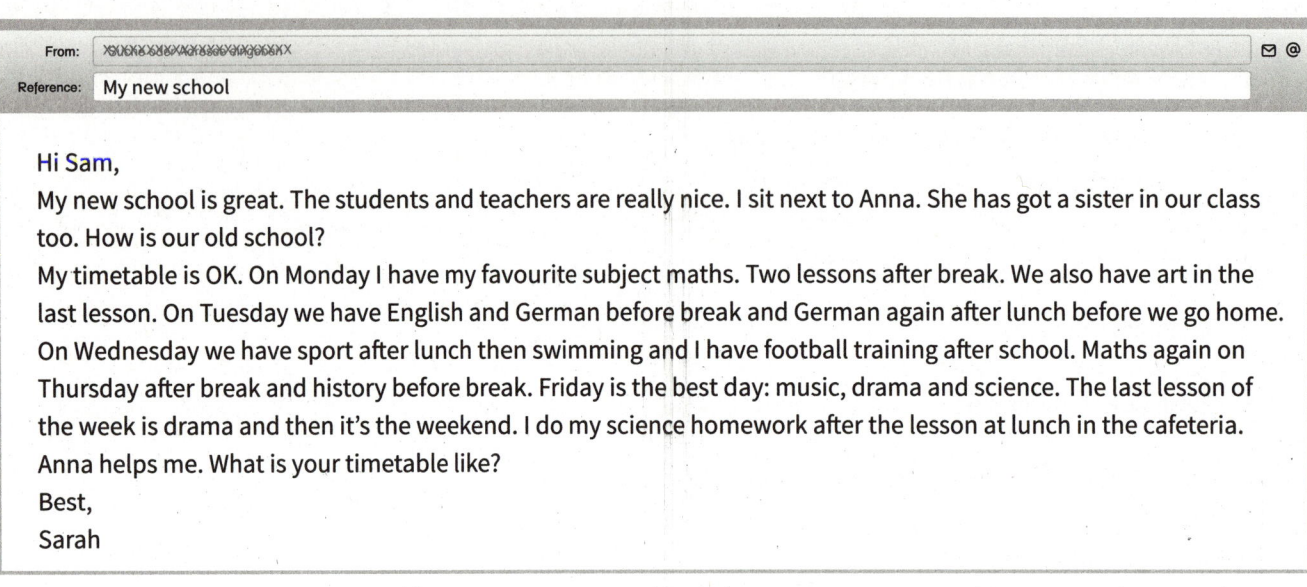

From: XⓍⓊⓄⓀⓍⓈⓊⓄⓍⓍⒶⓄⓍⓈⓈⓄⓋⓍⓄⓍⓆⓈⓈⓍXX

Reference: My new school

Hi Sam,

My new school is great. The students and teachers are really nice. I sit next to Anna. She has got a sister in our class too. How is our old school?

My timetable is OK. On Monday I have my favourite subject maths. Two lessons after break. We also have art in the last lesson. On Tuesday we have English and German before break and German again after lunch before we go home. On Wednesday we have sport after lunch then swimming and I have football training after school. Maths again on Thursday after break and history before break. Friday is the best day: music, drama and science. The last lesson of the week is drama and then it's the weekend. I do my science homework after the lesson at lunch in the cafeteria. Anna helps me. What is your timetable like?

Best,

Sarah

1 Answer Sarah's email

Write to Sarah about your timetable. Thank her for her email and ask her a question.

Schreibe Sarah eine E-Mail über deinen Stundenplan. Bedanke dich für ihre E-Mail und stelle ihr eine Frage.

Possible beginnings: Dear …,   Hi …,   Hello …,

Then: Thank you for …   Thanks for …   How are you?

_____

_____

_____

_____

_____

_____

_____

_____

Possible endings: Best wishes,   See you soon,   See you,   Best,   Take care,

2 Paul

a) Paul writes an email to his friend Mathew about his new school and timetable. Write Paul's email.
Paul schreibt seinem Freund Mathew eine E-Mail über seine neue Schule und seinen Stundenplan. Schreibe Pauls E-Mail.

Monday	Tuesday	Wednesday	Thursday	Friday
English	RE	history	English	music
German	sport	geography	maths	English
B	**R**	**E**	**A**	**K**
history	English	sport	history	geography
maths	science	English	geography	science
L	**U**	**N**	**C**	**H**
music	drama	maths	science	German
art	German	music	art	maths

Possible beginnings: Dear …,   Hi …,   Hello …,

Then: Thank you for …   Thanks for …   How are you?

_____

_____

_____

_____

_____

_____

_____

_____

_____

_____

_____

_____

Possible endings: Best wishes,   See you soon,   See you,   Best,   Take care,

Das englische Verb **have got** drück aus, dass jemand etwas besitzt oder etwas hat.
Es gibt zwei Formen: **have** und **has** sowie Kurzformen.
Bei der Verneinung verwendet man **not** oder eine Kurzform.

Personalpronomen	Langform	Kurzform	Verneinung	Frage
I, you, we, they	**have got**	**'ve got**	**have not got/haven't got**	What **have** you got?
he, she, it	**has got**	**'s got**	**has not got/hasn't got**	**Has** he **got** …?

Video: ▶ WEBCODE WES-121581-005

1 Forms of have got

a) Read the text and underline all the forms of *have got*. Don't forget the short forms.
Lies den Text und unterstreiche alle Formen des Verbs have got. Vergiss die Kurzformen nicht.

My name is Tom. We've got a dog. He has got three black legs
and one white leg. He is three. Have you got pets? We've got a big
white house. It has got a small garden. My family hasn't got a car.
Has your family got a car? We've got bikes. I've got a blue bike and
my brother has got a green bike. My parents haven't got new bikes
because they like their old bikes.

b) Match the sentences with the German meanings. The underlined parts of the text in a) can help.
Ordne die Sätze den deutschen Bedeutungen zu. Die unterstrichenen Textteile in a) helfen dir dabei

1. Wir haben ein Hund.
2. Er hat drei schwarze Beine.
3. Habt ihr Haustiere?
4. Es hat ein klein Garten.
5. Hat deine Familie ein Auto?
6. Wir haben Fahrräder.
7. Mein Bruder hat ein grünes Fahrrad.
8. Meine Eltern haben keine neuen Fahrräder?

A Have you got pets?
B Has your family got a car?
C We've got a dog.
D My brother has got a green bike.
E It has got a small garden.
F My parents haven't got new bikes.
G We've got bikes.
H He has got three black legs.

1	2	3	4	5	6	7	8
C							

2 Sentences

Complete the sentences with *have got, has got* ✔ or *haven't got, hasn't got* ✖ .
Setze have got, has got oder haven't got, hasn't got ein.

1. I _____ ✔ two sisters.

2. She _____ ✔ a black and white dog.

3. He _____ ✖ a black and white cat.

4. What _____ the dog _____ ?

   – The dog _____ ✖ a ball.

5. They _____ ✔ new bikes.

6. You _____ ✖ a great timetable.

7. She _____ ✔ geography on Friday.

8. We _____ ✖ a swimming pool in the garden.

3 What have they got?

Follow the lines and write sentences about the people.
Sieh dir die Bilder an und schreibe Sätze über die Personen.

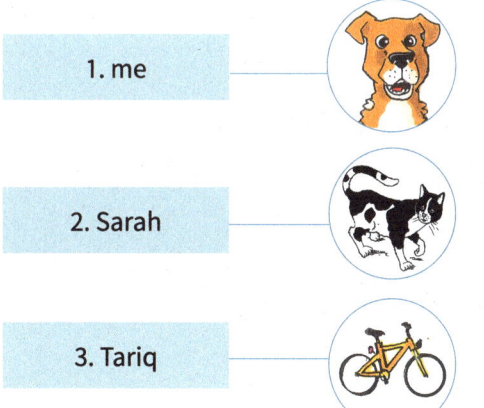

1. me

2. Sarah

3. Tariq

4. cat

5. Sarah + Tariq

1. I _____ .

2. She _____ .

3. He _____ .

4. It _____ .

5. They _____ .

Audio: (▶) WEBCODE **WES-121581-006**

1 Brendon's timetable

Listen to Brendon talk about his timetable. Are the sentences right or wrong? Tick ✔ .
Höre Brendonzu, wie er über seinen Stundenplan spricht. Sind die Antworten richtig oder falsch? Setze Häkchen.

	right	wrong
1. Brendon has 24 lessons a week.	☐	☐
2. He has a break at five past one.	☐	☐
3. One lesson is 45 minutes.	☐	☐
4. He has history on Mondays.	☐	☐
5. He doesn't like maths and PE.	☐	☐
6. He likes science.	☐	☐
7. He thinks history is boring.	☐	☐
8. School finishes at quarter past two.	☐	☐

2 Sam's email

From:	XXXXXXXXXXXXXXXXXXXXXXXXXXXXX	✉ @
Reference:	My timetable	

Hi Sarah,
Your timetable is great. I don't like my timetable. We have English every day with Mrs Jones. She is my tutor too.
Friday is good. We have sport in the afternoon and drama. Monday is OK because we have history and geography, my favourite subjects. On Wednesday I have got football training after school. That is good. When have you got football training?
Best,
Sam

Match the sentence parts.
Ordne die Satzteile zu.

1. Sarah's timetable	A Sam's tutor.
2. Sam has got	B history and geography.
3. Mrs Jones is	C is great.
4. Sam likes	D on Wednesday.
5. Sam's favourite subjects are	E Friday and Monday.
6. Sam has got football training	F Mrs Jones for English.

1	2	3	4	5	6
C					

3 Harry

Look at Harry's after school activities. Write his email to his friend.
Sieh dir an, welche Wahlfächer Harry nachmittags hat. Schreibe die E-Mail an seinen Freund.

Monday	Tuesday	Wednesday	Thursday	Friday
football	skateboarding	football	cooking	guitar lesson

Hi Dennis,

_____

_____

_____

_____

_____

Best,
Harry

4 Have they got …?

Complete the dialogue. Use forms of *have got.*
Ergänze den Dialog mit den richtigen Formen des Verbs have got.

name	thing
Flora	rabbit skateboard
Bob	cat skateboard
Harry	dog skateboard

Bob: _____ a dog, Flora?

Flora: No, I _____ . I _____ a rabbit.

Bob: _____ a dog?

Flora: Yes, he _____ . _____ a dog, Bob?

Bob: No, I _____ a dog. I _____ a cat.

Harry: _____ a skateboard, Bob?

Bob: Yes, I _____ a skateboard.

Harry: Flora _____ a skateboard too. Do you want to come to the skate park?

Bob: Yes, please. Thanks.

At home

Audio: ▶ WEBCODE WES-121581-007

1 It's not fair – Brendon and his jobs at home

Listen to Brendon. Who does he talk about? Write the people under the right jobs.
Höre Brendon zu. Über wen redet er? Schreibe die Personen unter die richtigen Pflichten.

| James | Brendon | Brendon's dad | Brendon's sister | Brendon's brother |

1.

_____

2.

_____

3.

_____

4.

_____

5.

_____

6.

_____

2 Right or wrong?

Are the sentences right or wrong? Tick ✔.
Sind die Sätze richtig oder falsch? Setze Häkchen.

	right	wrong
1. James lives in Liverpool.	☐	☐
2. Brendon likes helping around the house.	☐	☐
3. Brendon has to clean the toilet.	☐	☐
4. Brendon has a younger brother.	☐	☐
5. Brendon's family's rubbish bin is in front of their house.	☐	☐
6. Brendon never empties or fills the dishwasher.	☐	☐
7. Brendon's sister doesn't hoover Brendon's room.	☐	☐
8. Brendon will speak to James later.	☐	☐

3 Questions

Answer the questions.
Beantworte die Fragen.

1. What is it like in Liverpool? _____

2. Why does Brendon have to take out the rubbish? _____

3. Who fills the dishwasher? _____

4. Why doesn't Brendon's sister do it? _____

5. What pet has Brendon got? _____

6. What doesn't his sister hoover Brendon's room? _____

4 Mistakes

Find the mistake in each sentence and correct it.
Korrigiere die Fehler in den Sätzen.

1. Brendon has a big brother. _____

2. Brendon's sister fills the dishwasher. _____

3. Brendon feeds the cat. _____

4. Brendon will see James later. _____

Tipp

Um den Text besser zu verstehen, kannst du wichtige Textstellen unterstreichen. In dem Text unten beschreibt Paula ihre Wohnung. Unterstreiche die Zimmer und andere wichtige Orte im Haus.

My name is Paula and me and my family have got a new flat. It's amazing. Let me tell you about it. It's on the ground floor so we haven't got a balcony we have got a big garden. My cat loves the garden. There is a door to the garden from the kitchen and also from the living room. We have a big living room, and it is also the dining room. We sit at the table to eat breakfast and see the garden. My bedroom is on the left, next to the front door. It isn't very big, but there is room for my bed, desk and a wardrobe for my clothes. My older sister's bedroom is next to the kitchen. It is bigger than my room, but that's OK. Opposite my bedroom is my parents' bedroom. It is the biggest bedroom in our flat. The bathroom is next to my parents' bedroom. The toilet is between my bedroom and my sister's bedroom.

1 Paula's flat

Look at the plan Paula has drawn of her flat and label the rooms/places.
Schau dir den Grundriss von Paula's Wohnung an und beschrifte die Räume/Orte.

garden
kitchen	_____ / _____
_____	hall	_____
_____		
_____	front door	_____

2 Rooms and furniture

In Paula's description she writes about some furniture. Think of pieces of furniture that are usually in these rooms. Write the furniture in the lists.

In Paulas Beschreibung erwähnt sie auch verschiedene Möbel. Überlege dir, welche Möbel man normalerweise in diesen Räumen findet. Ergänze die Listen mit diesen Möbeln.

1. bedroom: bed, desk, wardrobe, _____

2. dining room: table, _____

3. living room: _____

3 Sentences

Complete the sentences with information from the text.

Vervollständige die Sätze mit den Informationen aus dem Text.

1. Paula and her _____ have got a _____ flat.

2. Paula's cat _____ the _____ .

3. Paula's family has _____ at the _____ .

4. Paula's _____ is next to the front _____ .

5. Paula has got a _____ for her _____ .

6. Paula _____ with her _____ and her parents.

4 Questions about the text

Answer the questions in complete sentences.

Beantworte die Fragen in ganzen Sätzen.

1. What does Paula think of the new flat? _____

2. Has Paula got a balcony or a garden? _____

3. How can you get to the garden? _____

4. Who has got the biggest bedroom? _____

5. Where is the toilet? _____

6. How many rooms are there in Paula's flat? _____

1 **What is in Max's bedroom?**

a) Write down the names of the things in Max's bedroom next to the right number below.

Schreibe die Namen der Gegenstände in Max' Zimmer zu den richtigen Zahlen.

1. _____

2. _____

3. _____

4. _____

5. _____

6. _____

7. _____

8. _____

9. _____

10. _____

11. _____

12. _____

b) Draw these things in Max's bedroom:

Zeichne diese Gegenstände in das Zimmer von Max:

| Max's school bag | a sofa | a TV | a bookcase |

2 Where are the things in Max's bedroom?

Use the prepositions to describe Max's bedroom.
Beschreibe das Zimmer von Max mithilfe dieser Präpositionen.

on	under	in	behind	above	between

1. There is a pencil case _____ Max's bed.

2. There is an apple _____ Max's desk.

3. Max's chair is _____ his bed and his desk.

4. There is a shelf _____ Max's bed.

5. There is a window _____ Max's desk.

6. Max's basketball is _____ his wardrobe.

7. There is a book _____ the shelf.

8. There is a CD _____ Max's desk.

> **Tipp**
>
> Sammle deine Ideen in einer Mindmap, einer Liste oder zeichne ein Bild, bevor du einen Text schreibst. Das hilft dir dann beim Formulieren deines Textes.

3 Your room

Write eight sentences about your bedroom. Use the sentences about Max's room to help you.
Schreibe acht Sätze über dein Zimmer. Die Sätze über das Zimmer von Max können dir dabei helfen.

1. _____

2. _____

3. _____

4. _____

5. _____

6. _____

7. _____

8. _____

Language Tip

Die einfache Gegenwart (*simple present*) verwendest du, wenn du über Gewohnheiten oder Dinge, die allgemein gültig sind, sprechen möchtest.
Verneinungen bildest du mit *don't* oder *doesn't*.
Für Fragen brauchst du *do* oder *does*.

Aussagen:	I **lay** the table on Fridays.	He often **empties** the dishwasher.
Verneinungen:	I **don't get up** at five.	She **doesn't get up** at five.
Fragen:	**Do** you **get up** at five?	What time **does** the cat **get up**?

! Bei **he**, **she** und **it** hängst du an das Verb ein **-s** an.

Video: ▶ WEBCODE WES-121581-008

1 The simple present

a) Read the text and underline all the forms of the simple present.
Lies den Text und unterstreiche alle Verben, die in der einfachen Gegenwart stehen.

I always get up 7 o'clock. On school days I have a shower and go downstairs. First, I feed my pets. They are very hungry. Then I make breakfast for everyone. My sister takes out the rubbish and my brother empties the dishwasher. We have breakfast together and then my parents fill the dishwasher. We all leave the house at 8 o'clock. After school I go to the park with my dog, and we play with his ball. He doesn't always listen, but he loves the park. My dad cooks dinner, and we all lay the table. We talk about our day. I don't do my homework until the evening. I don't go to bed very early. I watch TV or read a book before I sleep. What do you do every day?

b) Find the right sentences in the English text to match these German sentences.
Schreibe die richtigen englische Sätze aus dem Text auf, die zu den deutschen Sätzen passen.

1. Sie sind sehr hungrig. _____

2. Meine Schwester trägt den Müll raus. _____

3. Er hört nicht immer zu. _____

4. Ich gehe nicht so früh ins Bett. _____

5. Was machst du jeden Tag? _____

Donald's jobs	
make breakfast ✔	empty dishwasher ✔
feed cat ✘	fill dishwasher ✘
talk to the fish ✔	vacuum living room ✔
take out rubbish ✔	clean bathroom ✘
take the dog out ✘	cook dinner ✘

2 Sentences in the simple present

Complete the sentences about Donald's jobs. Use the *simple present*.
Vervollständige die Sätze über Donalds Aufgaben. Verwende die einfache Vergangenheit.

clean	cook	cook	do	empty	fill	take out	talk	go

make	not feed	not like	take	vacuum	not clean

I _____ breakfast for my family every day. I _____

the cat or _____ the dog out, but I _____

to the fish. My brother _____ those jobs. Before I

_____ to school, I _____ out the

rubbish and _____ the dishwasher. My sister _____ it, but she

_____ the dishwasher after breakfast. At the weekend I _____ the living

room and my brother _____ the bathroom. My sister _____ the dinner. I

_____ the bathroom or _____ dinner.

3 Questions in the simple present

Complete the questions and answers about Donald and his family.
Vervollständige die Fragen und Antworten über Donald und seine Familie.

1. _____ Donald _____ breakfast? – Yes, he _____ .

2. _____ his brother and sister _____ the rubbish? – No, they _____ .

3. Donald, _____ you _____ the dishwasher? – Yes, I _____ .

4. What _____ you _____ at the weekend? – I _____ the living room.

5. _____ your brother _____ the bathroom? – Yes, he _____ .

Audio: ▶ WEBCODE **WES-121581-009**

1 Rebecca's day

Listen to Rebecca. What does she do? Tick does or doesn't.

Höre Rebecca zu. Was macht sie? Setze Häkchen bei does oder doesn't.

	does	doesn't
1. goes to Hampton Court School		
2. brings her mum a cup of tea		
3. has breakfast with her family		
4. takes the bus to school		
5. likes English		
6. likes Mrs Taylor		
7. plays hockey		
8. has got a dog		

2 Hannah's house

I love our house. There are two bedrooms and a bathroom upstairs. The bedrooms are small but nice. They belong to me and my sister.

My parents sleep downstairs. Their bedroom is next to the living room. The living room is the biggest room. The kitchen, hall and a toilet are downstairs too. The kitchen is opposite the living room and is on the left of the front door. The toilet is next to the kitchen, also on the left. We haven't got a garden.

Read the text about Hannah's house. Which plan is right?

Lies den Text über Hannahs Haus. Welcher Plan stimmt?

A ☐

B ☐

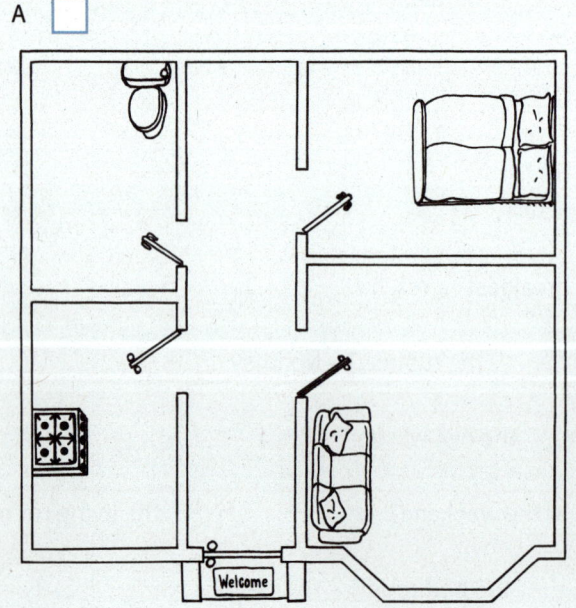

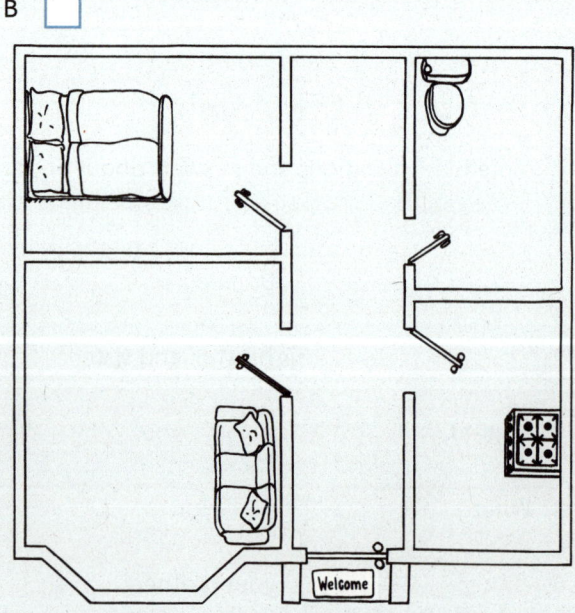

3 Mark's day

Write about Mark's day. Use the information in the box.
Schreibe über Marks Tag. Benutze die Informationen im Kasten.

Mark's day	
always make breakfast	sometimes fill dishwasher
often feed cat	not clean bathroom
not take out rubbish	never cook dinner

Mark always _____

_____

_____

_____

_____

_____

4 Me and my family

Complete the text with the right forms of the *simple present*.
Ergänze den Text mit den richtigen Formen der einfachen Gegenwart.

We all _____ jobs to do at home (have). My parents _____ up first and they _____ the

bathroom (get/use). My brother _____ up next (get). He _____ so long in the bathroom (spend).

I _____ in and out in five minutes (be). My dad _____ breakfast and my brother _____

the table (make/lay). My mum _____ the cat and I _____ the dog for a walk (feed/take).

After breakfast I _____ the dishwasher with the dirty cups and plates (fill). We _____ the house

together (leave). I _____ my bike to school, I _____ (ride/not walk). After school my brother

_____ the dishwasher and _____ the clean things in the cupboards (empty/put).

I _____ the living room and bedrooms (vacuum). My mum _____ dinner when she _____

home from work (cook/come). We _____ together and _____ about the day (eat/talk).

We _____ TV together and my brother _____ his homework (not watch/not do). What

_____ your family _____ every day (do)?

In town

Schau dir erst einmal die Bilder an, damit du weißt, auf welche Aktivitäten du beim Hören achten musst.

Audio: ▶ WEBCODE **WES-121581-010**

1 ## What can I do in my free time?

a) Which sports do Eleanor and Jacob talk about? Tick ✔️ .
Über welche Sportarten reden Eleanor und Jacob? Setze Häkchen.

1. ☐

2. ☐

3. ☐

4. ☐

5. ☐

6. ☐

b) Which sport does Eleanor choose? (Circle) it.
Für welche Sportart entscheidet sich Eleanor? Kreise das richtige Bild ein.

2 The right ending

Complete the sentences with the right ending.
Wähle die richtigen Satzenden aus.

1. Eleanor wants …
   a) a sport.
   b) a problem.
   c) more free time.

2. Eleanor isn't very good at …
   a) sport.
   b) hockey.
   c) swimming.

3. Jacob …
   a) plays hockey near his house.
   b) swims near his house.
   c) runs near his house.

4. Eleanor's library club ends at …
   a) 3 o'clock.
   b) 4 o'clock.
   c) 5 o'clock.

5. Eleanor can't go inline skating because …
   a) she doesn't like Jacob's friends.
   b) she hasn't got any skates.
   c) she hasn't got any time.

6. Eleanor can use … sticks and balls.
   a) her own
   b) Jacob's
   c) the club's

3 Missing information

a) Complete the missing information in the table.
   Vervollständige die Tabelle mit den fehlenden Informationen.

Sport	Place	Day	Time
swimming	swimming pool	Monday	
hockey	playing field		5 o'clock
tennis		Wednesday	3 o'clock
inline skating	park		afternoon
football (boys)		Friday	6 o'clock
football (girls)	gym	Tuesday	

b) What activities do you do? Write down what they are and when you do them.
   Was machst du in deiner Freizeit? Schreibe die Aktivitäten, die Wochentage und die Uhrzeiten auf.

Hey, Mark here, I want to tell you about my town. It's near London in England. I live here and my friends live here, too. We love our town. It isn't very big, but everything is here.

My favourite supermarket is in the town centre. I go shopping there with my mum on Fridays after school. We buy all the food we need. There is a market next to the playground on Saturdays so we get fruit and vegetables there.

I meet my friends in the park. We go there on our bikes. There is a bike shop in town next to my school. You can buy clothes in the new clothes shop. It's cool.

We haven't got a zoo, but there is a cinema. You can see all the new films there and they have fresh popcorn.

There is an old museum near the supermarket. It's free on Sundays.

There is a sports centre next to the swimming pool and a snack bar too.

1 What's missing?

Read the text. What is missing in the town? Draw it in the picture.

Lies den Text. Was fehlt der Stadt? Zeichne es in das Bild.

Tipp

Jetzt bearbeite diese Aufgaben zum Text. Du kannst hierzu auch noch weitere Textstellen markieren. Verwende eine andere Farbe.

2 Mark's town

Complete the sentences with places from the text.
Schreibe die richtigen Orte in die Lücken. Sie werden alle im Text genannt.

1. Mark goes to the _____ with his mum.

2. The _____ is on Saturdays.

3. Mark goes to the _____ on his bike.

4. The _____ is cool.

5. You can't see animals in a _____ in Mark's town.

6. You can have a burger at the _____ next to the _____ .

3 Questions about Mark's town

Answer the questions.
Beantworte die Fragen.

1. Where is Mark's town? _____

2. What does he buy in the supermarket? _____

3. Who does Mark meet in the park? _____

4. What shop is new in town? _____

5. What can you eat at the cinema? _____

6. What is free on Sundays? _____

4 Your town

Write three things that are in your town and also in Mark's town.
Schreibe drei Dinge auf, die es sowohl bei dir im Ort als auch in Marks Stadt gibt.

_____

_____

1 **In town**

a) Match the places with the activities you can do in them.
Ordne zu, welche Aktivitäten man an diesen Orten ausüben kann.

1. park	A read books
2. museum	B eat burgers
3. snack bar	C do lots of sports
4. swimming pool	D see animals
5. sports centre	E go to the skate park
6. library	F go swimming
7. supermarket	G buy food for the week
8. zoo	H learn new things

1	2	3	4	5	6	7	8
E							

b) Complete the text. Use the information from a).
Schreibe die richtigen Informationen aus a) in die Lücken.

I meet my friends in the _____ at the weekend. We take our skateboards

and go to the skate park. Next to the park is the _____ . We go swimming

there in the summer. We sometimes go to the _____ and look at the animals.

I like the elephants. We meet at the _____ after school and have a burger

and a drink. There is good music there, too. I don't like the _____ .

There are lots of things to read about old

things. The _____

is boring – too many books to read. The

_____ is great – football,

tennis, squash.

2 Funtown

a) **Look at the facts about Funtown.**
Schau dir die Fakten über die Stadt Funtown an.

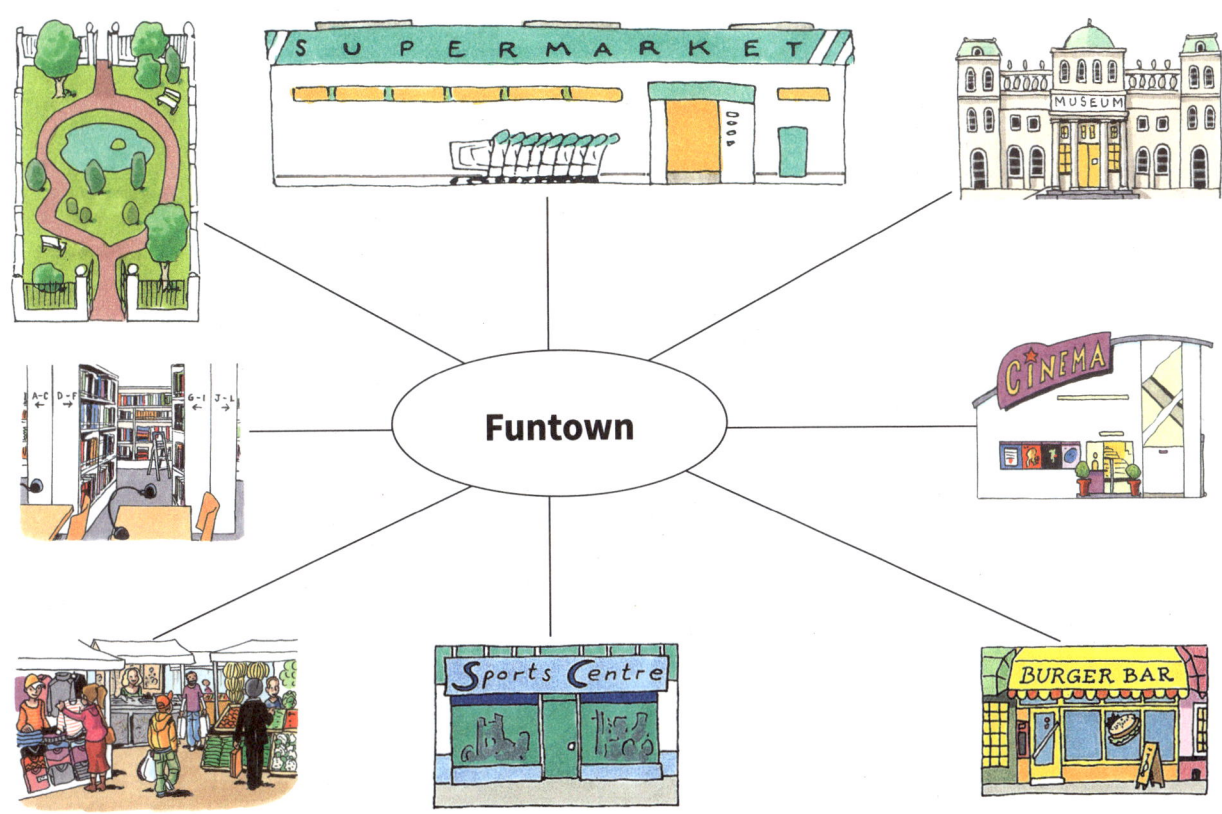

b) **Write about Funtown. Use the information from a) and use your ideas too.**
Schreibe einen Text über Funtown. Verwende die Informationen aus a) und deine eigenen Ideen.

Funtown is _____

_____

_____

_____

_____

_____

_____

_____

_____

Language Tip

Mit dem **Imperativ** (Befehlsform) forderst du jemanden auf, etwas zu tun.

Go home.
Open the window.

Wenn du möchtest, dass jemand etwas nicht tut, dann stellst du **don't** vor das Verb.

Don't go home.
Don't open the window.

Du solltest den Imperativ mit dem Wort *please* verbinden, sonst klingst du eher unhöflich.

<u>Please</u> open the window.
Don't open the window, <u>please</u>.

---

1 The imperative

a) Read the text and underline all the *imperatives*.
Lies den Text und unterstreiche alle Befehlsformen.

> The teacher is in the classroom. He talks to the class.
>
> "Sit down, please. Don't talk to your friends now. Take out your English books."
>
> "What page do we need?" asks Tom.
>
> "Turn to page 32, please." says the teacher. "Don't open the window, Sarah! It's too cold."
>
> "Sorry, Mr Smith."
>
> "Don't use your phones in lessons. Put them in your schoolbags."
>
> "Don't give us homework today, please. It's Friday."
>
> "OK. No homework today!"

b) Write the underlined sentences from the text in the table.
Schreibe die unterstrichenen Sätze aus dem Text oben in die Tabelle.

Was soll der Klasse tun?	Was soll der Klasse nicht tun?
Sit down.	

c) What should you do or not do in your classroom? Write two sentences with the *imperative*.
Was sollst du in eurem Klassenzimmer tun oder nicht tun? Schreibe zwei Sätze in der Befehlsform auf.

_____

_____

2 What can you do?

Look at the pictures. What do they tell you to do or not to do? Complete the sentences.

Schau dir die Bilder an. Was sollst du tun oder nicht tun? Vervollständige die Sätze.

1. _____ your book. (close)

2. _____ the window, please. (open)

3. _____ at the end of the road. (stop)

4. _____ page 1 in your English book. (turn to)

5. _____ in the library. (talk)

6. _____ in the river. (swim)

7. _____ football in the car park. (play)

8. _____ your dog in the sports centre. (take)

3 At home

Write two things your parents tell you to do or not to do.

Was sagen dir deine Eltern? Schreibe zwei Dinge auf, die du tun sollst oder nicht tun sollst.

_____

_____

Audio: ▶ WEBCODE **WES-121581-011**

1 Sophia's area

Listen to Sophia. What things are in her area? Tick ✔.
Höre Sophia zu. Was gibt es bei ihr in der Gegend? Setze Häkchen.

	in area	not in area
1. swimming pool		
2. lots of trees		
3. cars		
4. cinema		
5. shops		
6. restaurants		
7. park		
8. playground		

2 My town

My town is so boring. There are no good shops in the shopping centre. The clothes shop is for old people. The bike shop has expensive bikes. I don't like sweets so I never go in the sweet shop. The best shop in town sells my favourite cakes. The sports centre is new and you can go swimming, play football, meet your friends or eat in the snack bar there. I go to the cinema and the park with my friends. There is a new skate park in the park and they show all the new films at the cinema. My parents go shopping in the big supermarket not the small supermarket.

Are the sentences right or wrong? Tick ✔.
Sind die Antworten richtig oder falsch? Setze Häkchen.

	right	wrong
1. The shopping centre is good.	☐	☐
2. There is a clothes shop, a bike shop and a sweet shop.	☐	☐
3. The bikes aren't cheap.	☐	☐
4. There are two sports centres.	☐	☐
5. There isn't a place to go skateboarding.	☐	☐
6. There are two supermarkets.	☐	☐

3 Free time

Complete the text. Use the information in the box.
Schreibe den Text zu Ende. Verwende die Informationen aus dem Kasten.

sports centre:	swimming pool, football, gym, snack bar
shopping centre:	clothes, sweets, bikes
market:	clothes, fruit, vegetables, books
park:	skate park, playground, river

There is lots to do in town. You can go to the _____ and meet your friends at the snack bar. You

can play football in the _____ or go swimming in the _____ . I like the

shopping centre, too. You can buy so many things there. There are _____ shops and sweet

shops. There is a _____ shop with old bikes and new bikes. The _____ is

interesting. It also sells old things like books and clothes. You can buy fresh fruit and vegetables there, too.

The park is nice in the summer. There is a _____ and a _____ with boats.

Families like the _____ .

4 Bailey

Put the sentences in the right order to tell Bailey what he can or can't do.
Bringe die Sätze in die richtige Reihenfolge, um Bailey Befehle zu erteilen.

1. ! down sit Bailey,

   Bailey, sit down! _____

2. eat don't my homework, please !

   _____

3. your ball ! Bailey, get

   _____

4. It's hot. water Bailey, drink ! your

   It's hot. _____

5. bed, on sleep don't Bailey my !

   _____

Let's celebrate

Audio: ▶ WEBCODE WES-121581-012

1 At the shops

a) What food do Brendon and James need? Tick ✔.
Welche Lebensmittel benötigen Brendon und James? Setze Häkchen.

1. ☐

2. ☐

3. ☐

4. ☐

5. ☐

6. ☐

b) Write the words under the pictures.
Schreibe die Wörter unter die Bilder.

| chips | drinks | crisps | pizza | cake | cheese |

Tipp

Nicht vergessen: Du kannst den Hörtext vor jeder Aufgabe anhören. Nach jeder Aufgabe kannst du ihn noch einmal anhören, um deine Antworten zu überprüfen.

2 The right numbers

Complete the sentences with the right numbers.
Schreibe die richtigen Zahlen ausgeschrieben in die Lücken.

1. The boys need _____ pizzas.

2. The crisps are _____ pence for a big packet.

3. Sainsbury's is _____ minutes down the road.

4. The pizzas are _____ in Sainsbury's.

5. Brendon has got _____ pounds.

6. _____ pizzas are £1.50.

7. The boys need _____ pounds for the pizzas.

8. The boys have _____ pounds left for crisps, cake, extra cheese and vegetables.

3 Questions

Answer the questions. Make notes.
Beantworte die Fragen stichpunktartig.

1. Who has a birthday? _____

2. Has Brendon got drinks? _____

3. Where do they check where to go shopping? _____

4. What is good about the cake at Sainsbury's? _____

5. What are the pizzas like at Sainsbury's? _____

6. Who are always hungry? _____

7. How many pizzas do they want for each person? _____

8. What do they want to put on their pizzas? _____

Hey, my name's Samira and it's my birthday next week. I'm just planning what I need.

My party is in the garden. I want balloons in the trees and flowers on the tables. We have flowers in the garden, but I haven't got any balloons.

I want us to eat pizzas with cheese, ham and tomatoes on them. We have tomatoes in the garden, but I need to buy cheese and ham. Onions on a pizza are good, too. I need to buy onions from the market.

A chocolate birthday cake is the best. They have them in the supermarket. I don't need to make one I can buy one.

Everyone likes lemonade and orange juice, so I need to buy some. The drink's shop has my favourite lemonade. I don't want cola or milk. No one wants tea or coffee at my party.

We have biscuits in the kitchen cupboards and my friends are bringing their favourite crisps, so I don't need to buy them.

Have I got everything on my list?

1 Samira's list

Read the text. What does Samira need? Complete her shopping list.
Lies der Text. Was braucht Samira? Schreibe ihre Einkaufsliste.

Samira's shopping list

_____

_____

_____

_____

_____

_____

2 Where are the things?

Match the things with the places.
Wo sind diese Gegenstände? Schreibe die richten Buchstaben in die Tabelle.

1. ballons
2. flowers
3. tomatoes
4. onions
5. chocolate cake
6. lemonade
7. biscuits
8. crisps

A tables
B supermarket
C kitchen
D garden
E drink's shop
F trees
G friends' houses
H market

1	2	3	4	5	6	7	8
F							

3 Questions about Samira's party

Answer the questions.
Beantworte die Fragen.

1. When is Samira's birthday? _____

2. What grows in Samira's garden? _____

3. What does Samira want to eat? _____

4. What kind of cake does Samira want? _____

5. What doesn't anyone want to drink? _____

6. What are Samira's friends bringing? _____

4 Food and drink

Write down all the food and drink words from the text.
Schreibe alle Speisen und Getränke aus dem Text auf.

Food words: _____

Drink words: _____

> **Tipp**
> Wenn du eine Bild beschreiben möchtest, schau dir das Bild genau an. Am besten fängst du von oben oder unten an, wenn du das Bild beschreibst.

1 In the supermarket

Look at picture and complete the text.
Schau dir das Bild an und ergänze die fehlenden Informationen im Text.

This is a picture of a supermarket. There are _____ people in the supermarket.

A _____ is looking at the pizzas. A man is looking at the _____

and some bananas. There are lots of shelves in the supermarket. _____ there are two

fridges with milk, meat and cheese. _____ there are drinks. I can see orange juice,

_____ and cola. _____ there are sweets, crisps, cakes, biscuits and

muesli. There is a man _____ of the picture. He is wearing a _____

sweatshirt. There is a girl _____ of the picture. She has a blue bag and is wearing a

_____ sweatshirt, a blue skirt and pink trainers.

2 Playing a game

a) Look at the picture.
   Schau dir das Bild an.

b) Describe the picture. Use the words below and your own ideas.
   Beschreibe das Bild. Verwende die Wörter und deine eigenen Ideen.

| play a game | drink | people | lemonade | chairs | table | pictures |

There are _____

_____

_____

_____

_____

_____

_____

_____

Mit der **Verlaufsform der Gegenwart** (*present progressive*) drückt man aus, was jemand gerade tut oder was gerade passiert. Die Ereignisse sind noch nicht abgeschlossen.

Vergangenheit	Gegenwart	Zukunft

Die Verlaufsform wird gebildet mit einer Form von **be (am/is/are)** und der **ing-Form des Verbs.**

Aussagesatz:	I am talking to you.	They are eating pizza.
Verneinung:	I am not talking to you.	They aren't eating pizza.
Fragen:	Why are you talking to me?	Are they eating pizza?

Video: (▶) WEBCODE WES-121581-013

1 The present progressive

a) Read the text and underline all the *present progressive* forms
Lies den Text und unterstreiche alle Verben, die in der Verlaufsform der Gegenwart stehen.

It's a nice day and there are lots of people in the park. Let me tell you what <u>they are doing</u>.

There is a man selling ice creams. They look yummy.

Two girls are riding their bikes. They are wearing blue helmets.

Six boys are playing football. The red team isn't winning.

A man is taking his big dog for a walk. He is talking to a woman with a small dog. They aren't laughing. The small dog is barking at the big dog.

A family is eating a picnic. They are sitting on the grass next to the lake. They are celebrating a birthday.

b) Answer the questions. Use the underlined parts in the text.
Beantworte die Fragen. Verwende hierzu die unterstrichenen Textteile.

1. What is the man selling? _____

2. What are the girls wearing? _____

3. What are the boys playing? _____

4. What are the dogs doing? _____

5. Where are the family? _____

6. What are the family doing? _____

2 What is happening?

Complete the sentences with the verbs in brackets in the *present progressive*.
Setze die Verben in Klammern in die Verlaufsform der Gegenwart.

1. The boy _____ (talk) to a clown.

2. The clown _____ (do) lots of tricks.

3. The woman _____ (not smile) at the clown.

4. The children _____ (laugh).

5. The woman _____ (give) the children ice creams.

6. The children _____ (not watch) the clown now.

3 What are they doing?

Look at the pictures. What are they doing? Complete the sentences.
Schau dir die Bilder an. Was machen die Menschen gerade? Schreibe die Sätze zu Ende.

| play a guitar | not eat ice cream | look at jeans | sing a song | not read a comic |

1. The girl _____ .

2. The man _____ .

3. The children _____ .

4. The people _____ .

5. The girl _____ .

Audio: ▶ WEBCODE **WES-121581-014**

1 **Sarah's dream birthday party**

Are the sentences right or wrong? Tick ✔.
Sind die Sätze richtig oder falsch? Setze Häkchen.

	right	wrong
1. Sarah invites her friends from school.	☐	☐
2. The party is from the afternoon until 10 o'clock.	☐	☐
3. There is a small party in the garden.	☐	☐
4. Sarah's family joins the party in the evening.	☐	☐
5. Sarah hasn't got any cousins.	☐	☐
6. Her aunt and uncle sing a birthday song.	☐	☐
7. They watch films of Sarah as a baby in the evening.	☐	☐
8. Sarah gives her friends presents.	☐	☐

2 **My party**

Sam:	It's my party on Saturday – please come.
Anna:	Sure. What time is it?
Sam:	It 3 o'clock in the afternoon, in my garden. Do you know my address?
Anna:	Yes, it's number thirteen Main Road.
Sam:	Great! It's my birthday. Please bring food for the party, no presents.
Anna:	OK. What about a potato salad?
Sam:	Yes, please. There is a motto too.
Anna:	Do I need a costume?
Sam:	No, the motto is summer.
Anna:	That's fun. See you on Saturday. Bye.

Read the text. Which is the right invitation for the party? Tick ✔.
Lies den Text. Welche Einladung ist die richtige? Setze ein Häkchen.

1. ☐   2. ☐

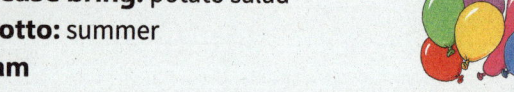

PLEASE COME TO MY PARTY!
When? Saturday, 3:00 a.m.
Where? 13 Main Road, in the garden
Why? my birthday
Please bring: potato salad
Motto: summer
Sam

PLEASE COME TO MY PARTY!
When? Saturday, 3:00 p.m.
Where? 13 Main Road, in the garden
Why? my birthday
Please bring: food for the party
Motto: summer
Sam

3 Shopping for a party

Look at the shopping list. Complete the dialogue with the right food.
Sieh dir den Einkaufszettel an. Schreibe die richtigen Lebensmittel in die Lücken.

Ben:	Hi Peter. We need to go shopping for my party.
Mo:	No problem. I can help. What do you need?
Ben:	I want to make pizzas. We need _____ ,
	_____ , _____ , ham, …
Ben:	I have _____ . We don't need to buy it.
	We need something to drink, too.
Mo:	What about _____ and orange juice?
Ben:	Lemonade is my favourite drink. We need to buy some. We have lots of orange juice.
Mo:	What about a cake? Do you want to make one?
Ben:	Yes, a chocolate cake. We need _____ , _____ , flour,
	sugar and _____ for the cake.
Mo:	Do we need to buy everything?
Ben:	No. We have _____ and _____ in the cupboard.

> **Shopping list**
> eggs
> salami
> lemonade
> butter
> chocolate
> tomatoes
> cheese
> milk

4 At the party

What are the people doing at the party? Use the *present progressive.*
Was machen die Personen auf der Geburtstagsfeier gerade? Verwende die Verlaufsform der Gegenwart.

not eat	sing	sit	walk	walk	not dance

1. The dog _____ under the table.

2. The cat _____ on the fence.

3. The children _____ Happy Birthday.

4. The girl _____ to the song.

5. A girl _____ in a wheelchair.

6. The friends _____ cake.

On holiday

1 The United Kingdom

Write the names in the right places on the map.
Schreibe die Namen an die richtigen Stellen der Karte.

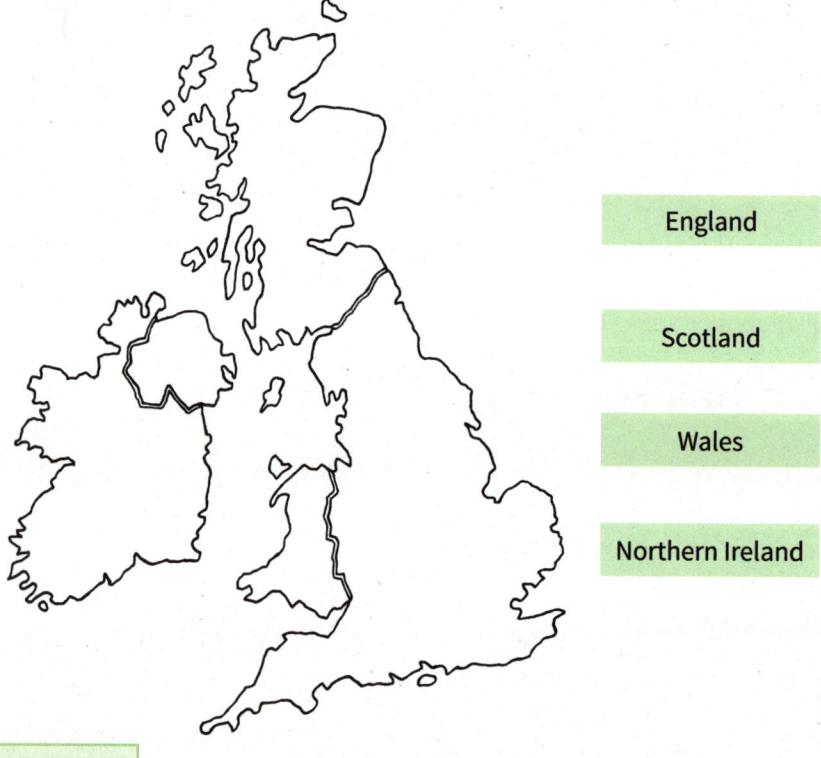

England

Scotland

Wales

Northern Ireland

Audio: ▶ WEBCODE **WES-121581-015**

2 The weather today

Are the sentences right or wrong? Tick ✔.
Sind die Sätze richtig oder falsch? Setze Häkchen.

	right	wrong
1. The weather won't be good today and tomorrow.	☐	☐
2. The hottest place is in the southwest of England.	☐	☐
3. The temperatures might be 25 degrees.	☐	☐
4. The temperatures aren't warm for this time of year.	☐	☐
5. It will be cloudy in Northern Ireland.	☐	☐
6. There will be strong winds in Scotland.	☐	☐
7. There will be rain in the morning.	☐	☐
8. Tomorrow will be a nice day for everyone.	☐	☐

Tipp

Nicht vergessen: Du kannst den Hörtext vor jeder Aufgabe anhören. Nach jeder Aufgabe kannst du ihn noch einmal anhören, um deine Antworten zu überprüfen.

3 Complete the sentences.

Complete the sentences with the right words.
Vervollständige die Sätze mit den richtigen Worten.

1. The weather will be perfect in most parts of _____ .

2. The temperature will be between _____ .

3. The weather is warm for this time _____ .

4. There will be winds on Scotland's _____ .

5. There will be rain in _____ .

6. Temperatures will be better _____ .

7. Don't forget to _____ .

8. You can also enjoy a wonderful day in _____ .

4 What's the weather?

Match the weather with the right place. There is more than one weather description for each place.
Ordne das Wetter dem richtigen Ort zu. Es gibt mehr als eine Wetterbeschreibung für jeden Ort.

A lots of sun
B 18-22 degrees
C extremely warm
D cloudy
E stronger winds
F rain in the afternoon
G 14 degrees
H nice and sunny day

1. England
2. Wales
3. Scotland
4. Northern Ireland

1	2	3	4

Tipp

Es gibt nicht viel Platz auf eine Postkarte, aber man möchte oft vieles sagen.

Hi Mark,

We're on holiday here in Brighton. The weather is great.
No clouds or rain, just the sun.
We go to the beach every day. Yesterday me and
my sister built a sandcastle. We have some new
friends, Sarah, Paul and Noah. We meet them on
the beach every morning and have fun all day.
The food is good. We eat fish and chips every day on
the beach. They taste amazing.
See you on Saturday.
Anna

Mark Smith
32 Main Road
Lewisham
LM32 1XY

1 Anna's postcard

a) Read the postcard. Which picture matches Anna's postcard?

Lies den Text. Welches Bild passt zu Annas Postkarte?

1. ☐   2. ☐   3. ☐

b) Which picture matches the weather in Brighton?

Welches Bild passt zum Wetter in Brighton?

1. ☐   2. ☐   3. ☐

Tipp

Jetzt bearbeite diese Aufgaben. Lies die Postkarte noch einmal, um sicher zu gehen, dass du noch alles weißt.

2 About the postcard

a) Are the sentences right or wrong? Tick ✔ .
Sind die Sätze richtig oder falsch? Setze Häkchen.

	right	wrong
1. Mark is on holiday in Brighton.	☐	☐
2. The weather is great.	☐	☐
3. They go to the beach every day.	☐	☐
4. Anna and her sister built a sandcastle yesterday.	☐	☐
5. They have made four new friends.	☐	☐
6. They meet them on the beach in the afternoon.	☐	☐
7. They eat fish and chips every day.	☐	☐
8. Anna will see Mark on Saturday.	☐	☐

b) Write the corrected sentences from a) here.
Verbessere die falschen Sätze von Aufgabe a).

_____

_____

_____

3 Questions about the postcard

Answer the questions. Write complete sentences.
Beantworte die Fragen. Schreibe vollständige Sätze.

1. What is the weather like in Brighton? _____

2. Where does Anna go every day? _____

3. What did she build on the beach? _____

4. What are the names of her new friends? _____

5. What does she eat every day? _____

6. Where does she eat every day? _____

Tipp

Wenn du eine Postkarte schreiben möchtest, denke daran, dass du nicht so viel Platz hast.

1 A postcard

a) Put the parts of the postcard in the right order.
Bringe die Sätze in die richtige Reihenfolge.

A See you at the weekend.

B I'm having a great time here, but we have to leave on Friday.

C Today we went on a boat trip on the Thames.

D Hi Sue,

E I'm going to the Tower of London.

F Rosie

G Tomorrow we are going to the Science Museum.

H I'm on holiday with my family in London.

1	2	3	4	5	6	7	8
D							

b) Write the postcard in the correct order.
Schreibe den Text der Postkarte richtig auf.

_____

_____

_____

_____

_____

_____

_____

_____

_____

_____

2 Your postcard

a) Look at the information about a holiday.
   Schau dir die Informationen über den Urlaub an.

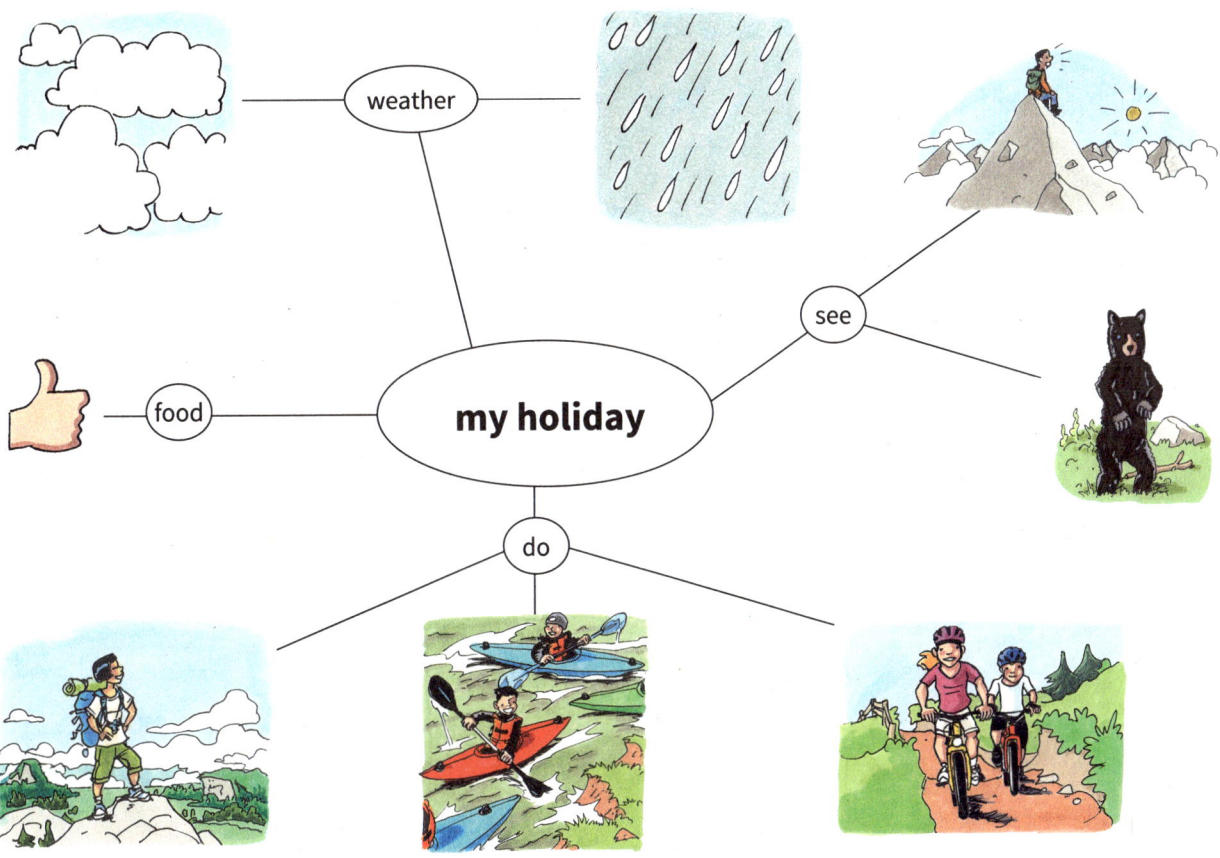

b) Write a postcard to your friend. Use the information from a) and use your ideas too.
   Schreibe eine Postkarte an einen Freund/ihre Freundin. Verwende die Informationen aus a) und eigene Ideen.

Hi _____

_____

_____

_____

_____

_____

_____

_____

Das **simple past** verwendet man, wenn man über abgeschlossene Ereignisse in der Vergangenheit reden möchte.

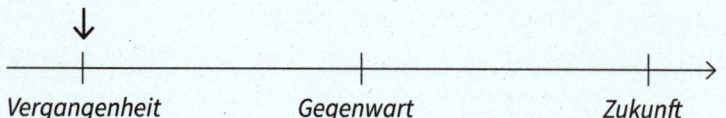

Vergangenheit   Gegenwart   Zukunft

Bei den regelmäßigen Verben bildet man die Vergangenheitsform, indem man ein **-ed** an das Verb anhängt.

play → played   **walk → walk**ed

Die unregelmäßigen Verben haben eine eigene Form, die man lernen muss.

		Endet das Verb mit einem -e, dann hängst du nur ein -d an (z. B. like**d**). Endet das Verb auf einen kurzen betonten Vokal und einen Konsonanten, dann wird der Konsonant verdoppelt (z. B. stop**ped**).
Aussagesätze:	**He played football yesterday.**	
Verneinung:	**He didn't play football yesterday.**	
Fragen:	**Did he play football yesterday?**	

Video: ▶ WEBCODE WES-121581-016

1 The simple past

a) Read the text and underline all the verbs in the *simple past*.
Lies den Text und unterstreiche alle Verben, die in der einfachen Vergangenheit stehen.

I <u>had</u> a great weekend. We went to the mountains for the weekend. We arrived on Friday evening and had a great meal. We all slept really well and got up early on Saturday morning. We got dressed and had a big breakfast. Then we took the bus and walked up a mountain. It was a lovely day and there was a lovely view from the top of the mountain. We decided to come down the mountain in the cable car. On Sunday we met my aunt and uncle and cousins, and we went kayaking all day. We all enjoyed the day together. We came home tired but very happy.

b) Find the *simple past* forms of these verbs in the text.
Schreibe die richtigen Vergangenheitsformen aus dem Text auf.

1. have: _____   7. walk: _____

2. go: _____   8. be: _____

3. arrive: _____   9. decide: _____

4. sleep: _____   10. meet: _____

5. get up: _____   11. enjoy: _____

6. take: _____   12. come: _____

2 What happened?

Underline the correct form of the verb. The signal words help you.
Unterstreiche die richtige Verbform. Die Signalwörter helfen dir dabei.

1. I wash/washed my hair **yesterday evening**.
2. My older brother leaves/left school **last year**.
3. We go/went on holiday to London **every year**.
4. **Last year** we move/moved to Scotland.

5. The train **always** arrives/arrived late.
6. I fall/fell off my bike **last week**.
7. They play/played football **on Mondays**.
8. **Last summer** we stay/stayed at home.

3 What did Ben do or not do yesterday?

Put the verbs in the *simple past*.
Setze die Verben in die einfache Vergangenheit.

1. Yesterday Ben _____ (get up) late.

2. He _____ (not eat) breakfast before school.

3. He _____ (forget) his English homework.

4. His English teacher _____ (not shout) at him.

5. Ben and his friends _____ (be) really hungry at lunchtime.

6. His class _____ (play) football in PE after lunch.

7. After school, he _____ (not miss) the bus, it _____ (be) late.

8. Ben _____ (go) to the cinema with his friends yesterday evening.

4 Questions for Emma

Write the questions that go with the answers.
Schreibe die passenden Fragen zu den Antworten.

1. When did you eat your breakfast? _____ I ate my breakfast **at 7 o'clock.**

2. _____ We watched TV **in the living room.**

3. _____ **Yes, I phoned** my dad.

4. _____ **No, I didn't feed** the dog.

5. _____ I went to school **by bike.**

6. _____ After school, I **visited my grandma.**

7. _____ **I helped my mum** in the evening.

8. _____ I read a story to **my sister.**

Audio: ▶ WEBCODE WES-121581-017

1 Sophia's holiday

What does Sophia take on holiday? Tick ✔.
Was nimmt Sophia in den Urlaub mit? Setze Häkchen.

	yes	no
1. green trousers		
2. green T-shirt		
3. a dress		
4. a shirt		
5. a sweatshirt		
6. a jacket		
7. trainers		
8. hat		

2 Paul's holiday

Hi Clare,

I'm on holiday in Wales. The weather is awful.

We didn't see the sun, only clouds and rain all week.

We went hiking yesterday. We got very wet. Today

we went hiking and also got very wet. ☺

The food is good. We eat lots of different things.

We have a big breakfast: sausages, bacon, toast

and eggs. I don't need any lunch.

See you on Friday.

Paul

Clare Jones
32 North Street
Leeds
LE123ZY

Read the postcard and answer the questions. Write complete sentences.
Lies die Postkarte und beantworte die Fragen. Schreibe vollständige Sätze.

1. Where is Paul? _____

2. What is the weather like? _____

3. What are the two activities he writes about? _____

4. What happened at both activities? _____

5. What is the food like? _____

6. What does Paul eat for lunch? _____

CHECK On holiday

3 A postcard

Complete the postcard. Use the information in the box.
Ergänze die fehlenden Informationen im Text. Sie stehen alle im Kasten.

weather:	OK; sun and wind
see:	museums, queen
food:	not very good
do:	walking, boat trip

We had a great holiday in Scotland. The weather was _____ . There was

_____ and _____ , but we did lots of things. I

_____ the food in the hotel. It wasn't very good. We saw lots of things in Scotland.

We went to three _____ : a science museum, a car museum and a clothes

museum. We saw the _____ when we went to a farm show. We did lots of

_____ and we went on a great _____ . We saw lots of things

from the river. It was great.

4 Yesterday

What did the people do yesterday? Use the *simple past*.
Was haben die Menschen gestern gemacht? Verwende die einfache Vergangenheit.

do	not rain	stay	go	meet	not see	have	be

1. We _____ on a camping holiday.

2. It _____ .

3. The weather _____ good.

4. I _____ a boy. His name is Robert.

5. We _____ on a big campsite.

6. We _____ lots of barbecues.

7. We _____ any dogs on the campsite.

8. We _____ lots of fun activities.

Bildquellen

|Alamy Stock Photo, Abingdon/Oxfordshire: amana images inc. / Pholdar nine/a.collectionRF Titel; Borges Samuel 31.1. |Alamy Stock Photo (RMB), Abingdon/Oxfordshire: Mainka, Markus 11.1; WILDLIFE GmbH 12.1. |Shutterstock. com, New York: Jagodka 43.1. |stock.adobe.com, Dublin: aerogondo 51.3; ekaphon 51.2; irishasel 51.1; Mediteraneo 51.4; nelen.ru 13.1; thaninee 51.5; valiza14 9.1.

Trackliste

Alle Audios und Videos können auf der Homepage www.westermann.de/webcode mit dem im Heft vermerkten Webcode (z.B. WES-121581-001) abgespielt werden. Dies funktioniert auch auf einem Smartphone oder Tablet.

Kapitel	Seite	Aufgabe	Webcode
1	4	1	WES-121581-001
1	10	Language tip	WES-121581-002
1	12	1	WES-121581-003
2	14	1	WES-121581-004
2	20	Language tip	WES-121581-005
2	22	1	WES-121581-006
3	24	1	WES-121581-007
3	30	Language tip	WES-121581-008
3	32	1	WES-121581-009
4	34	1	WES-121581-010
4	42	1	WES-121581-011
5	44	1	WES-121581-012
5	50	Language tip	WES-121581-013
5	52	1	WES-121581-014
6	54	1	WES-121581-015
6	60	Language tip	WES-121581-016
6	62	1	WES-121581-017